THE COMPLETE PLANTING DESIGN COURSE

PLANS AND STYLES
FOR EVERY GARDEN

THE COMPLETE PLANTING DESIGN COURSE

PLANS AND STYLES
FOR EVERY GARDEN

HILARY THOMAS

STEVEN WOOSTER PHOTOGRAPHY AND DESIGN

MITCHELL BEAZLEY

This book is dedicated to the memory of my parents who
encouraged and nurtured my love of the natural world.

Hilary Thomas

First published in Great Britain in 2008 by
Mitchell Beazley, an imprint of Octopus Publishing Group Limited,
2–4 Heron Quays, London E14 4JP.
An Hachette Livre UK company
www.hachettelivreuk.co.uk

Distributed in the U.S. and Canada by Octopus Books USA:
c/o Hachette Book Group USA
237 Park Avenue
New York NY 10017

A CIP catalogue record for this book is available from the British Library.

ISBN: 978 1 84533 412 3

Commissioning Editor: Helen Griffin
Art Director: Tim Foster
Art Editor: Victoria Burley
Designer: Anne Wilson
Project Editor: Georgina Atsiaris
Editor: Joanna Chisholm
Proofreader: Jo Murray
Production: Lucy Carter
Index: Sue Farr

Set in Adobe Garamond and Univers
Printed and bound in China by Toppan Printing Company

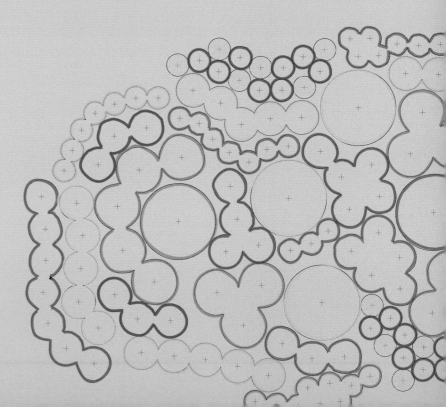

contents

3 plant selection

4 planting plans

5 styles and themes

6 aspects of business

foreword

I suppose my love of flowers began as a young child when my father would take my sister and me for walks along the country lanes. We would always attempt to name the flowers we saw in the woods and hedgerows, and my plant knowledge quickly grew. At university I studied biological science, which included some botany and ecology, yet it was not until I acquired my own garden that I – like many others – became obsessed with cultivated plants. At that point I decided to retrain in horticulture.

From that time my view of plants and planting changed as I began to see plants not as things to collect but as design material that needed to be carefully selected for

its form, texture, and colour. I can still remember that first lesson on planting with John Brookes when he said, "take out half of what you have put in and double up on the rest", a wonderful piece of advice that I still pass onto my students at Capel Manor.

Over the years students have asked for all course handouts to be produced as a book, so that is what I have done here. It should prove of value to every keen gardener, whether working in their own garden or professionally for clients large and small.

When visiting gardens open to the public it is often disappointing to find so little good planting design. The beds and borders are full of a wonderful array of plants but there appears no order or structure. Planting is highly subjective, personal, and dynamic, and this is what makes it so hard. Although new ideas are now appearing in our public gardens and landscapes, change is likely to be slow as long as few gardeners and horticulturalists are taught the theory of planting design.

Hilary Thomas

For many people it is the pleasure of gardening that first attracts them into growing and learning about plants. It is all too easy though to have a garden full of impulse purchases, which presents itself as a restless plant collection rather than a well-thought-out design with a sense of unity and wellbeing. Learning how to select a plant for its visual qualities, in the same way as you choose wallpaper or furniture when designing a room, is an important stage in understanding planting design. You also need to know how to implement these principles of design.

1 planting design

plant form

The form of a plant is its overall shape when in leaf. This has the greatest visual impact and plays a much more significant role in planting composition than any individual feature such as leaf shape or flower colour. A plant's form can be affected by environmental conditions especially light and wind exposure. In a wood, for example, trees may lose their natural form and develop tall spindly shapes because they compete for light.

Similarly hawthorn trees growing on an exposed coastal site take on strange windswept shapes because the buds on the windward side become desiccated by the cold salt-laden wind.

Although plant form is wonderfully varied, plants can be grouped into a number of main categories, and each of these has an individual role in composition.

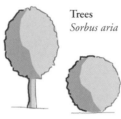

Trees
Sorbus aria

Shrubs
Choisya ternata

ROUND FORMS

Round is a formal shape. A loose round does occur naturally in some trees and shrubs such as whitebeam (*Sorbus aria*) or Mexican orange blossom (*Choisya ternata*), while other plants such as yew and box can be clipped to this shape. A round shape is a strong one and creates a sense of security or containment. It can be used as a full stop at the end of a border or as a focal point in a more informal planting.

DOME OR HUMMOCK FORMS

Many plants develop a dome or hummock, and they are excellent for softening the edge of a border. Try for example smaller herbaceous plants such as geraniums, heucheras, and alchemilla. This very relaxed form is also invaluable for visual stability and for linking plants within a composition. In trees a dome or hummock form can be seen in hawthorn (*Crataegus persimilis* 'Prunifolia') and English oak (*Quercus robur*) and in shrubs such as hebe, *Viburnum davidii*, and lavender.

Trees
Ilex aquifolium
Sophora japonica

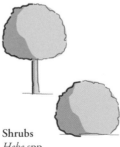

Shrubs
Hebe spp.
Santolina chamaecyparissus

Punctuation marks

LEFT The shaped forms of box act as visual full stops at the edge of the patio and provide an eye-catching contrast with the softer forms in the rest of the garden.

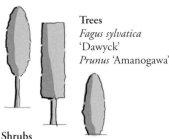

Trees
Fagus sylvatica
'Dawyck'
Prunus 'Amanogawa'

Shrubs
Ilex crenata 'Fastigiata'
Juniperus scopulorum 'Skyrocket'

COLUMNAR OR CYLINDRICAL FORMS

This form, which is rare in wild plants, is the outline shape produced by trees and shrubs with a fastigiate habit (see p.20), in which all the branches ascend and make a shape similar to an exclamation mark. A columnar or cylindrical form is usually triggered by a genetic change in the species, and it is then selected for propagation. Examples in trees are Italian cypress (*Cupressus sempervirens*), Lombardy poplar (*Populus nigra* 'Italica'), and Rock Mountain juniper (*Juniperus scopulorum* 'Skyrocket'). The columnar form is a very strong shape, and when used among other plants can be assertive, making an eye-catching focal point. It should be used with restraint though, because wrongly placed it can be an eyesore. The form becomes less dramatic and more stable if used as a group of three or five plants. Many herbaceous plants such as acanthus and aconitum exhibit this form in their flower spikes.

FAN OR SPIKY FORMS

The fan can be an open graceful form, making it a useful shape for a tree in a small garden because it allows plenty of space for planting underneath. A pair of fan-shaped trees can make an attractive informal arch. In shrubs it often becomes a very strong shape when large spiky leaves combine to give the plant an architectural or sculptural quality, as seen in *Mahonia* x *media* 'Charity' and *Phormium tenax*. The spiky fan becomes dramatic and aggressive, so creating a focal point or accent plant in the planting scheme. Less dramatic spiky fans can be seen in ferns such as shuttlecock fern (*Matteuccia struthiopteris*) and in herbaceous plants such as *Sisyrinchium striatum* and flag iris (*Iris germanica*). Fans and spiky forms need to be given enough space in a planting scheme to show off their eye-catching forms. The spiky shape does not often occur naturally in temperate garden plants; it is most often found in hotter climates so looks most at home in an exotic planting scheme with large foliage and vibrant colours.

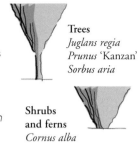

Trees
Juglans regia
Prunus 'Kanzan'
Sorbus aria

**Shrubs
and ferns**
Cornus alba
Matteuccia struthiopteris

Trees
(when clipped)
Liquidambar styraciflua
Taxus baccata

Shrubs
Chamaecyparis lawsoniana cultivars
Ilex aquifolium

Shrubs
Danae racemosa
Rosa moyesii

CONICAL FORMS

This fairly formal shape is often found in young trees and in most older conifers. It is normally taller than it is wide and can be used to add a striking accent to a planting scheme. A conical form is more stable and subtle than a columnar shape, although very dark conical trees such as yew can seem rather austere.

ARCHING FORMS

Many plants begin growing vertically or in a fan shape but as they mature their leaves or branches become heavy and arch over, taking on a softer form. Such plants need sufficient space in a border for their leaves or branches to arch, otherwise the plants develop a loose domed form. Many of the bamboos and shrub roses develop an arching form, as do *Buddleja davidii* and *Danae racemosa*. It can also be seen in many herbaceous plants and grasses.

IRREGULAR FORMS

Some plants grow naturally in a loose irregular and sometimes quirky way, so creating a varied and unpredictable outline. Such irregularity can look good when viewed against the strong geometry of buildings or the open skyline. In trees an irregular form can be seen in Scots pine (*Pinus sylvestris*) and cedar of Lebanon (*Cedrus libani*) and in shrubs in the tiered habit of *Cornus controversa*.

Trees
Cedrus libani
Pinus sylvestris

TRAINED FORMS

Many plants can be shaped into quite unnatural forms by training or clipping. Shrubs can be shaped into square hedges, and trees such as lime (*Tilia*) and hornbeam (*Carpinus*) can be pleached, so creating a "hedge on legs". These forms are strongly geometric and allow plants to play the part of an architectural feature such as a wall, normally achieved only with bricks and mortar. They bring a sense of order and rhythm and can create a backdrop for softer features such as an herbaceous border or reinforce the axes and layout of the garden.

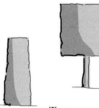

Trees
Carpinus spp.
Tilia spp.

flower form in herbaceous plants

When selecting trees, shrubs, and ground cover plants it is the overall form of the plant that is important. Many herbaceous plants do not have strong forms as they emerge, and it is the actual forms of the flowers and the following seedheads that are of prime importance to the gardener or designer. The accompanying foliage texture and colour should also be considered. Herbaceous plants are also far more dynamic than trees and shrubs, and their form changes dramatically as the seasons progress. Flower heads come in a variety of forms, and plantings based on these shapes will be more successful than those reliant on just colour. Piet Oudolf – the Dutch designer and nurseryman – has already categorized the flower forms of herbaceous plants in his book *Designing with Plants* so those same categories will be used here.

SPIRES AND SPIKES

These very strong flower forms are similar to the cylindrical or columnar outlines of trees and shrubs (see p.13). They are at their best used in a drift or group at the back of the border, where their eye-catching shape will be seen to good effect. Some such as *Acanthus mollis* have a single spire while others such as the veronicastrums (left) have several branching spires, creating a softer candelabra-like effect.

BUTTONS AND SPHERES

This group covers a wide array of different forms from the tight spheres seen in echinops to the shaggy whorls of monarda and the button-like heads of astrantias (above). In all of them the concentrated cluster of flowers is tightly packed, making the heads stand out against a softer background. They are less dominant than spires and are often used midborder to create a strong drift of flower form and colour.

PLUMES

Plumes are generally soft and create a foamy cloud-like effect. They can be used to link the stronger flower forms in the same way that hummocks and medium textures connect the stronger forms and textures in the border. Examples of plumes are the thalictrums, plume poppy (*Macleaya cordata*), and sea kale (*Crambe cordifolia*) (right).

DAISY-LIKE FLOWER HEADS

Daisies seem to have an air of simplicity about them, perhaps because they remind us of childhood and making daisy chains on sunny afternoons. The flowers tend to grow on closely packed stems, creating a mass of colour. Some flower heads such as on echinaceas develop on stiff branching stems while others such as on asters (right) and heleniums are more lax and may require staking. Many provide late summer and autumn colour. Like umbels, they can be used to link the stronger flower forms.

SCREENS AND CURTAINS

These flowers are light and airy, and can create a net-curtain effect in the border, allowing you to see through them to stronger forms and colours. Because of their transparent qualities they can be used to give height at the front or middle of the planting and conjure exciting visual displays. Examples of screen and curtain plants are *Verbena bonariensis* (right) and giant feather grass (*Stipa gigantea*).

UMBELS

These are the domes and hummocks of the flower world, and their gently rounded forms ground the taller more energetic spires and globes. Many closely resemble the wild flowers – such as cow parsley and Joe Pye weed (*Eupatorium purpureum*) (above) – found in hedgerows and meadows, and so lend an air of naturalism to the planting. Fennel (*Foeniculum vulgare* 'Giant Bronze') and *Sedum* 'Herbstfreude' produce umbels.

texture

Everyone is familiar with the term texture when applied to fabrics or surfaces, but they may be new to the idea that texture also matters when selecting plants. Many of you may have stroked the wonderful woolly leaves of lambs' ears (*Stachys lanata*) or run your fingers through the silky leaves and flowers of the feather grass *Stipa tenuissima*. What you are doing is checking the texture of the leaves and flowers, confirming how you think they should feel.

When considering texture you usually think of it as a "touchy feely" sensation, but it can also be defined as the visual roughness or smoothness of an object. In fact by feeling the object you are confirming the visual analysis you have already made about its texture.

Plant texture can therefore be defined as the visual roughness or smoothness of any part of a plant. When seen from a moderate distance a plant's visual texture is affected by the size, shape, and surface of its leaves. Depending on these three characteristics, a plant is normally referred to as having coarse, medium, or fine texture.

Coarse texture

Large leaves and stout twigs have the coarsest texture, and examples with these attributes are *Gunnera manicata*, Bergenia, and Indian bean tree (*Catalpa bignonioides*). Such coarse-textured plants catch the eye because their leaves are very visible at a distance. Each leaf tends to break up the outline and

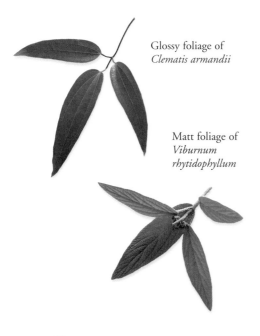

Glossy foliage of
Clematis armandii

Matt foliage of
*Viburnum
rhytidophyllum*

Fine textures

LEFT Plants with fine texture are usually those with the smallest leaves, although larger leaves that are finely divided as with this fern can also be said to be fine textured. Their light airiness can create considerable contrasts with plants of the same or another texture.

Leaf surface

FAR LEFT The surface of a leaf is another visual tactile experience and adds to the sensory pleasures that plants offer. Look at a leaf for its light-reflective qualities. Is it glossy or matt or in between? A glossy leaf such as on *Clematis armandii* will reflect light and make a plant appear nearer than a matt-leaved one such as *Viburnum rhytidophyllum*.

distract attention from the plant's overall form. Because they become strong focal points and foreshorten a space, coarse-textured plants can overpower a small garden, and too many make the space seem claustrophobic.

A sense of greater depth can be achieved by placing coarse-textured plants in the foreground and placing finer-textured ones around the boundaries. In a small garden this could mean planting *Fatsia japonica* near the house and a fine-leaved shrub such as *Osmanthus* × *burkwoodii* at the end of the garden.

Medium texture

Medium-textured plants are used to link the coarse- and fine-textured plants, so helping to unify a planting scheme and soften the contrast between coarse and fine textures. Many evergreen shrubs such as *Viburnum tinus*, Portugal laurel (*Prunus lusitanica*), and *Elaeagnus* × *ebbingei* possess medium texture, as do herbaceous plants such as geraniums and heucheras.

Fine texture

The finest-textured plants are those with the smallest leaves or leaflets. Examples are *Hebe rakaiensis*, yew (*Taxus baccata*), box (*Buxus sempervirens*), and feather grass (*Stipa tenuissima*). Such plants tend to be easy to look at and do not demand attention in the way that coarse-textured plants do. They give the impression of being at a greater distance than a coarse-textured plant, and they appear to recede within the field of vision. Planting a small garden with a high proportion of fine-textured plants will make the space seem larger than when filled with more coarse-textured plants.

Some fine textures such as those on fennel leaves or the flowers of gypsophila are light, airy, and expansive. Other fine-textured plants such as clipped spheres of box take on strong forms because the individuality of each leaf is lost and the outline of the plant becomes the dominant feature. Fine-textured plants can therefore play an important role in formal planting schemes, especially when trimmed into geometric shapes. Clipped yew makes the most wonderful fine-textured backdrop to ornamental planting.

Bold performer
ABOVE *Gunnera manicata* has huge leaves and very coarse texture, making it a wonderful focal plant next to water.

Texture affects form
ABOVE Fine-textured plants have a strong form; coarse-textured ones are looser.

LEAF SHAPE AND SURFACE

Leaves offer a satisfying range of different shapes, and these play a significant role in the overall texture. Leaves can be oval, heart-shaped, linear, palmate, huge and rounded, or small and narrow – the range is endless. The margins can be smooth, serrated, toothed, or spiky. All of these characteristics contribute to the overall visual texture of the leaf.

Helleborus argutifolius

Cornus alba 'Aurea'

Hebe perfoliata

Griselinia littoralis

Ficus carica

Acer saccharinum

Eucalyptus pauciflora subsp. *debeuzevillei*

The importance of form and texture in planting design

When you first start to design with plants the task seems almost overwhelming; there is so much to consider. A good plant knowledge is invaluable, and you should visit as many gardens as you can, taking with you a camera and a note- or sketchbook to record any plant associations that you find successful. Don't worry if you cannot identify all the plants, because this can be done at home later with some good reference books. Learn to be analytical, asking yourself why a plant association works. Look at the forms and textures within the group and sketch them.

Strong forms such as columnar or spiky fans and coarse or bold textures are all dramatic and stimulating, while domes, hummocks, and fine textures are restful and unimposing. If there is too much dramatic or stimulating planting it becomes chaotic, while too many restful and unimposing forms results in a dull planting. It is therefore important to get the balance of these qualities right when combining plants for best effect. This can also be explained by saying that the more exciting plants have higher visual energy than the more restful ones. These high-energy plants will all fight for attention. To appreciate the qualities of each of these individual plants they need to be complemented or grounded with areas of visually less demanding planting.

You will always need a good variety of the softer forms, domes, and hummocks in any planting scheme.

Contrasting forms and textures
LEFT The strong form and coarse texture of the phormium demand attention in this border and provide dramatic contrast to the strongly grounding forms of the clipped box and santolinas. The low-growing *Prunus laurocerasus* 'Otto Luyken' on the slope behind the phormium repeats the fan shape and its dark shiny foliage contrasts well with the fine texture and strong forms of the box.

Effective repetition

LEFT The clipped planting around the trees reflects the rectangles of the walls and architecture, while the strong santolina domes in the foreground are repeated in softer forms behind by lavender and *Perovskia atriplicifolia*.

Compatible plants

BELOW Creating planting groups so that individual plants look well with their companions needs thought. All the plants must thrive in the particular growing conditions, whether hot and dry or damp and shady, so that they look like a natural community. Then they must work well together visually in terms of forms, texture, and colours.

DOMINANT OR BLAND?

A plant grouping in which one shape is repeated in different sizes and quantity can also work well provided there is one dominant leader. The spiky form is repeated at different scales in the group below.

The spiky shape of the mahonia is strong and dominates the grouping.

When the Mahonia is removed, the scale and drama change and the group becomes bland.

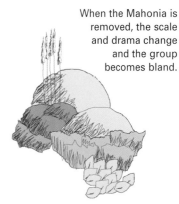

Group of three
A vertical, round, and spreading form create a restful triangle.

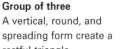

Group of five
The vertical is firmly anchored here by round and horizontal forms.

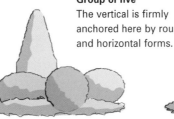

Group of five
The grouping also works well with a dominant fan-shaped plant.

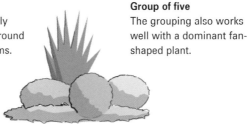

Imagine the planting

RIGHT Before selecting any plants try to visualize and sketch your planting scheme simply as forms and textures. Once you have done this you can then choose the plants that will give you the sketched effect.

winter framework

The importance of habit

The way that a tree or shrub develops its woody framework – the arrangement of its branches – is known as its habit. Many trees and shrubs do not have a strong identifiable habit. In those that do, it can often be seen best in winter when the branches are bare.

Trees and shrubs with well-defined habits make good focal points because the tracery of bare branches in winter is still strong enough to demand attention and be interesting.

FASTIGIATE HABITS
All the branches grow upwards in a fastigate habit, and this gives rise to the strong columnar or cylindrical form found in trees such as *Pyrus calleryana* 'Chanticleer' (above). It can be a useful habit for street trees, where space may be limited. Some trees such as the fastigiate hornbeam take on a much broader spreading habit as they mature.

TORTUOUS HABITS
Plants with a tortuous habit have arisen as genetic mutations and have been selected for this characteristic, such as contorted hazel and tortured willow (*Salix babylonica* var. *pekinensis* 'Tortuosa') (above). Plants with a tortuous habit can be difficult to place and are best used on their own as a focal point and are very effective near rocks or water.

WEEPING OR PENDULOUS HABITS

All the branches droop from the main stem in a weeping habit. This lovely shape has a restful line, creating serenity and peacefulness. It can also appear heavy, because the weeping branches draw attention to the ground, so the presence of a light lively element such as water is the perfect complement. A less dramatic habit, known as pendulous, is seen in silver birch (*Betula pendula*), in which the main branches grow upwards and only droop down at the branch ends.

HORIZONTAL HABITS

The branches are held at right angles to the main stem in a horizontal habit. This creates a calm and restful scene. Horizontal lines provide visual stability, and planting with low-growing shrubs such as the horizontal junipers will ground the more exciting vertical elements of a planting scheme. Shrubs such as dogwood (*Cornus controversa*) (above) and *Viburnum plicatum* as well as trees such as majestic cedar of Lebanon (*Cedrus libani*) establish a strong visual impact as focal points or accent planting.

ARCHITECTURAL OR SCULPTURAL PLANTS

Some plants have such strong forms or textures that they are best defined as being architectural or sculptural; they bring a year-round presence to the garden. It may be their form or coarse texture, or both, that creates this strong presence. Such plants include trees such as umbrella pine (*Pinus pinea*), exotics such as the banana *Musa basjoo* (above), the tree fern *Dicksonia antarctica*, palms such as Chusan palm (*Trachycarpus fortunei*), and cloud-pruned plants such as Japanese holly (*Ilex crenata*). They are often most success in a modern-style or minimalist garden, where the other planting is very low key.

SKETCHING HABITS

The best season to appreciate the framework of a deciduous tree or shrub is in winter, when the branches are bare, and this is a good time to photograph or practise sketching them as well. A tortuous habit looks particularly beautiful after a light snow fall. When clad in foliage during summer, a tree with a strong habit can still have an identifiable form.

Weeping habit

Pendulous habit

Tortuous habit

Horizontal habit

Fastigiate habit

colour

Colour appreciation is very subjective. The colours you choose to use in any planting scheme will be affected not only by your own likes and dislikes but also by the location, style, mood, and use of the garden as well as its aspect and light. The hardest gardener perhaps to please is the one who "wants lots of colour", finds foliage and structural planting dull, and is unable to see that green is also a colour. Colour is usually transient, changing with the seasons, so it is really important that form and texture are not forgotten in the rush to think about "colour".

What then is colour? The colour we perceive is due to the presence of particular pigments that absorb or reflect certain wavelengths of light. When all the wavelengths are reflected, the eye sees this as the colour white, and when all are absorbed it is called black. Leaves appear green because chlorophyll reflects the green light rays, and similarly bluebells seem blue-violet because the pigment in the flowers throws back the blue-violet light rays. The colour perceived also depends on the quality and brightness of the light in which it is viewed as well as the texture and form of the plant.

Perceiving colours

RIGHT In this arrangement of chairs the eye is drawn immediately to the red chair at the front, then it moves to the yellow one behind, and then across to the blue and green chairs, so reinforcing how the eye perceives the hot and cool colours. Hot colours draw your attention and advance towards you, so making a space seem smaller, while the cool ones are undemanding and recede away from you, making a space appear larger.

Red is a hot colour that demands your attention and seems to come towards you rather than receding into the background.

Yellow is less demanding but still appears to come forward, reflecting available light.

Green is a cool and undemanding colour and makes a wonderful foil for the other colours.

Blue is a very cool colour that appears to move away from you and almost merges with the background.

indigo

violet

red

orange

yellow

green

blue

The rainbow

LEFT This consists of seven colours. In a colour wheel, however, you will find the three primary colours – red, blue, and yellow – and the three secondary colours – orange, green, and violet – but not indigo, even though it appears in the rainbow itself.

THE COLOUR WHEEL

The spectrum, which we see when a rainbow forms, is nature's way of arranging colours in order. When bent round to make a circle, it forms the colour wheel. Such a wheel will help you understand the relationship between different colours. A very simple guide is well worth making, or you can buy a colour wheel from an art shop.

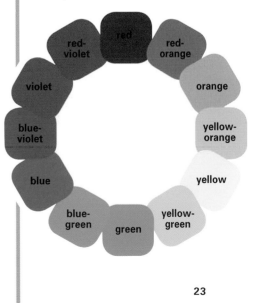

red-violet

red

red-orange

violet

orange

blue-violet

yellow-orange

blue

yellow

blue-green

yellow-green

green

Understanding colours

The three primary colours of red, blue, and yellow are the essential colours from which all other colours are derived. Each of the secondary colours of green, orange, and violet is a mixture of two primaries and lies between the relevant primaries on the colour wheel (see p.23). Green is produced by mixing blue and yellow; orange by combining red and yellow; and violet by merging blue with red. Further colours, the tertiaries, are created on either side of each secondary by mixing the primary and secondary together. These tertiary colours simply take the name of the two colours on either side, so for example on either side of orange would be the tertiaries yellow-orange and red-orange. You can further enlarge this range of colours by making tints, tones, and shades of colour. Think of a paint colour chart and the seemingly endless range of colours from which to choose.

Hot colours

When viewing the colour wheel it is possible to understand how colours fall into two distinct categories. The reds and oranges, which are in one part of the wheel, are known as "warm" or "hot" colours, while the greens and blues, which are in the other half of the wheel, are termed "cool" colours. Hot colours are strong, stimulating, and lively, but they can also be harsh and strident. Plants from sunny climates such as the tropics or South Africa tend to produce flowers in hot colours. In their natural habitat the intensity of colour is enhanced by the strong sun, so when used in temperate climates plants need to be placed in full sun otherwise they look either garish or washed-out and dull.

Hot colours also become dark and difficult to spot in the evening or in poor light. Because they are strong colours they can also be distracting, and by demanding attention they appear to advance towards you, so making a space seem smaller. Hot-coloured plants need to be used with care in a small garden, otherwise like coarse texture they can make the space feel claustrophobic. Famous hot-coloured plantings include the Red Border at Hidcote Manor, in Gloucestershire, UK, where vibrant reds are used with purple foliage and touches of violet, and the Hot Garden at Great Dixter, in Sussex, UK, where they are combined with exotics such as bananas and cannas. Many "hot" herbaceous flowers perform late in the year, so hot borders and gardens are best visited in the late summer or autumn.

A hot border
FAR LEFT This border at The Old Vicarage, Norfolk, UK, provides late summer excitement especially when the flowers are combined with purple foliage and coarse texture. The strong colour of the red dahlias at the front of this hot border (and illustrated left) really pull your eye into the planting.

Setting the mood

ABOVE Dogwoods create the backdrop for this woodland garden, where the cool colours of geraniums and aquilegias are supported by soft lime-green fringe cups (*Tellima grandiflora*) and white foxgloves. Thus colour can be used to reinforce the mood and style of the planting scheme.

Cool colours

The colours of indigenous flowers in northern Europe are fairly subdued. Soft spring colours – pale blue, creams, and pinks – give way to stronger colours as the seasons progress. The cool colours – blues, pale violets, and greens – look best in shade and show up well in evening light. They produce a restful calming effect. Blue in particular can be difficult to spot and can create what appears to be a void in a planting scheme.

Cool colours appear to recede, thus making a space feel larger. They are therefore ideal in a small garden or when trying to conjure the illusion of space. A closely cut lawn (fine texture and cool colour) will always make a garden seem larger than an equivalent area planted up with brightly coloured flowers and foliage.

TINTS, SHADES, AND TONES

Starting with a hue such as red, great variations in colour are produced by adding black, grey, or white.

a HUE + white = a TINT
eg, red + white = pink

a HUE + black = a SHADE
eg, red + black = maroon

a HUE + grey = a TONE
eg, red + grey = plum

These tints, shades, and tones "lurk" behind their parent hues and, to a greater or lesser extent, share their characteristics. The range of colours that can be created is therefore seemingly endless.

Colour and light

Colours change through the day as the sun moves through the sky. At sunrise and sunset the light has a warm glow of red or orange, and the hot flower colours glow in such a light. Cool colours, however, become washed out, because there is little blue light for them to reflect. By midday the light becomes almost white, the hot colours lose their glow and seem washed out, while the cool colours appear revived. Once the sun has gone down the hot colours disappear, while the cool colours and white continue to be visible in the dim conditions.

The quality of light also changes with the seasons. In winter the light is grey and cold, and the palest of winter blossoms and flowers will glow – for example, snowdrops or winter-flowering cherry. Spring sunlight is warmer and stronger, new leaves are lime-green, and flower colours tend to be yellow, blue, and violet. In summer the light becomes stronger, and the traditional English border of pinks, blues, and greys looks lovely on a grey cloudy day but in intense light can look very flat. The dominant colour is green, both foliage and grass, and yellow and violet or the hotter reds can look wonderful on a sunny day.

In autumn the light is golden, and the predominant colours are the reds and golds of flowers and foliage. The blues and violets of michaelmas daisies and species asters produce good contrast at this time of year.

Spring
The pale pink cherry blossom stands out in late-winter and early-spring light.

Autumn
The golden seedheads of the grasses glow in golden light, evoking meadows of ripe corn.

Soft sunlight
RIGHT The warm soft morning light at Hadspen, Somerset, UK (right) and the evening light in France (far right) enhance the gentle colours of nepeta and lavender, which seem to glow.

spring

summer

Summer
The heat haze of summer at Giverny, France, was the inspiration for Monet and his vibrant use of colour in some paintings.

autumn

winter

Winter
An early frost in Beth Chatto's garden in Essex, UK, casts a cold blue light, cooling down the warm shades of autumn.

EMOTIONAL RESPONSE

Everyone probably has a palette of colours they enjoy wearing or they choose when decorating the house. Research has shown that colours can evoke subconscious emotional responses, and particular colours are now used in hospitals and prisons to reduce stress and create restful environments. The following list suggests some emotional responses to certain colours.

Red warm, exciting, and passionate – red roses and hearts, as on St Valentine's Day.

Orange a restless active colour that should be used sparingly as a hue and more generously as a tint (apricot) or shade (rust).

Yellow cheerful, lighthearted, bright, spring-like. Pale yellow is excellent for brightening dark areas.

Green cool, refreshing, healthy, relaxing. An excellent foil for all other colours (green lawn).

Blue cool, serene, although too much can be chilly or depressing.

Violet regal, striking, dignified. Care should be taken not to overuse it in structural planting because violet can look dowdy and depressing, especially in late summer.

White cool, uplifting, clean. Use sparingly as a highlight in a border to intensify other colours.

Grey/Silver can be mysterious and delicate. Excellent as a background instead of green.

Colour schemes

The two most important approaches to selecting colour in the garden – using harmonious colours or contrasting ones – are best understood by studying the colour wheel (see p.23). Harmonious colours are those that are adjacent or near each other on the wheel: for example, blue, violet, and blue-green from the cool side of the colour wheel; or red, yellow, and orange from the warm side.

Harmonious colour schemes

When dominated by blues or colours with a blue bias such as violet, planting schemes are subtle and restful. Silver-green and blue-green foliage also work well, keeping the combination together. Cool harmonies also look at their best in shade, and as night descends they linger longer than the dark colours. Pinks can also be included in the cool harmonies, providing you choose a cool pink and not a warm one.

Pinks and reds can move into either part of the colour wheel. Those reds that are crimson and the pinks derived from them all have a touch of blue in them and so associate well with cool colours, while those reds that are derived from vermilion and the associated pinks all tend to have a touch of yellow in them and so look good when placed with the warmer colours.

Harmonies using colours from the hot part of the colour wheel are very powerful and vibrant and can easily eclipse the other plantings in a garden so it is best to keep them separate. The Hot Garden at Great Dixter, Sussex, UK, is enclosed by a hedge, which makes it all the more dramatic. Hot colours can also be toned down by the introduction of purple-leaved plants such as cotinus, hazel, or pittosporum, but these should be used sparingly otherwise the garden can look dark and gloomy particularly in late summer. Most hot borders are late-season performers so this is another reason for placing them in a separate part of the garden.

Really dramatic use of harmonizing colours is achieved in planting schemes with hues as adjacent masses. Colours should not be diluted by introducing a variety of tints, tones, or shades.

Harmonizing colours

LEFT At the RHS garden Hyde Hall, in Essex, UK, drifts of blue-violet nepeta blend with bold plantings of *Erysimum* 'Bowles' Mauve' and the spheres of *Allium hollandicum* 'Purple Sensation'. Lime-green euphorbia flowers add a touch of sharpness to this otherwise gentle planting.

Complementary colours

RIGHT The vivid colours of eryngiums and heleniums are from opposite sides of the colour wheel, and thus produce a strong complementary colour scheme.

Monochromatic colour schemes

Another way of devising a harmonizing colour scheme is to use the tints, tones, and shades of one particular hue. A very famous monochromatic scheme is the White Garden at Sissinghurst Castle in Kent, UK, where tints, tones, and shades of white flowers are offset by silver and green foliage contained within clipped box hedges. Old-fashioned shrub and species roses in an array of sombre reds, carmine, pinks, and dusky rose are also possible in a monochromatic colour scheme.

Contrasting colour schemes

Colours from opposite sides of the colour wheel create contrasting colour schemes. The strongest differences are between those colours that are exactly opposite each other on the wheel – red with green; blue with orange; yellow with violet – and these are then called complementary colours.

A complementary colour makes up for everything that its opposite colour is lacking. By placing complementary colours next to each other, each colour stimulates the eye to see the other colour more intensely. Therefore blue will look more intense next to orange, and red will appear brighter when positioned next to green.

The use of complementary colours also involves hues selected from both the warm and the cool parts of the colour wheel, whereas harmonious colour schemes are usually close together on the wheel, that is, the colours are of a similar colour temperature.

Split complementary

In a split complementary colour scheme, the colours on either side of a complementary colour are selected, instead of the complementary colour itself. So, for example, yellow is used with blue-violet and red-violet instead of violet, and red is placed with blue-green and yellow-green.

Triad scheme

In this type of contrasting colour scheme three colours equidistant on the colour wheel are chosen. Red, blue, and yellow – the three primaries – are very exciting to use and can be seen in the red poppies, blue cornflowers, and yellow corn marigolds found in summer meadows. Similarly the three secondary colours – orange, green, and violet – could be adopted.

Split complementary
ABOVE Yellow is seen here with strong blue-violet delphiniums and the softer pink/red-violet of ageratum in this split complementary colour scheme.

Not quite a triad
ABOVE This plant grouping is close to being a triad scheme. The red and blue, however, are not true hues, and they are dominated by the strength of the yellow.

Antagonistic colours

Colours that are antagonistic are said to clash. Some people think that the colours of nature cannot clash, and indeed most European native plants are relatively gentle in colour and are frequently diluted with greens and soft buffs, making a tapestry of colour. In gardens, however, colours tend to get used in bolder drifts and blocks, and many of the plants come from hotter climates so the colours are deeper and more intense than those of temperate native flowers. The colour shocks and clashes come from the reds, pinks, and oranges. The reaction between them is because some reds are blue based and so move towards the cool colours while others are yellow based and move towards the hotter part of the colour wheel. The clashes come when a red that has blue in it is placed with orange, or when a pink that has a blue content is used with yellow or a yellow-based red. Some people find these colour clashes exciting, while others shy away from them. These colour shocks, however, can be fun in the right situation. Most need the intense light of the tropical sun to be really effective, and a large space such as a park where games and activities are taking place. They would be too disruptive and out of place if introduced in a small garden.

WHITE IN THE GARDEN
White can play a variety of roles within a planting scheme. Few flowers are truly white: most have a touch of blue, green, or yellow and so can be matched with plants of the appropriate colour. White flowers with a solid silhouette such as lilies or tulips tend to stand out among other colours and can therefore disrupt a strong colour scheme. Plants that have small foamy flowers such as *Crambe cordifolia* can add a touch of mystery like a net curtain at the back of a border. Silver, grey, or white-variegated foliage also associates well with white flowers. Dark shady areas can be lightened by the use of shrubs and herbaceous plants that produce white or cream flowers.

Antagonistic colours

LEFT In this group of primulas the blue-based pinks and reds clash with the yellow so creating a very vibrant but antagonistic colour scheme.

Strong white

BELOW LEFT The white in this bed is very dominant, drawing the eye and breaking up the planting.

Anything but white

BELOW When there is no white splitting the group, as here, the planting is perceived as an entity.

principles

It is impossible to imagine a world without plants: they create the ceilings, walls, and floors of outdoor spaces. In rural landscapes, trees and hedges break up the land, reinforcing the wonderful patchwork pattern of the fields. In the garden they add the third dimension, reinforcing the character and mood of the design. Getting the planting right is very much harder than designing the layout of the space. Once paving is laid it hardly changes, just weathering with age. Planting on the other hand is dynamic, developing from day to day, season to season, and year to year. Apart from the practical considerations of soil and aspect there are all the design qualities of the site and the plants to be planned. It is no wonder then that much of the planting around you is little more than a collection of plants.

Before choosing any plants it is really important to draw up a brief so that you are completely clear in your own mind what it is that you are trying to achieve. In order to be successful you then need to follow some design principles very similar to those you would consider when designing the layout of the space.

The importance of unity

Unity means oneness or things being similar, having a strong link between them. In planting this can be achieved in a variety of ways – in styling, in moods or themes, in details, and in the way the site is situated.

Unity of style

A garden should have a definable style, which may be formal, informal, or somewhere in between, and it is important that the planting reinforces this style. The planting of a formal modern roof garden may be restricted to bamboo and clipped box, while an informal country cottage garden could have drifts of colourful herbaceous plants and shrub roses.

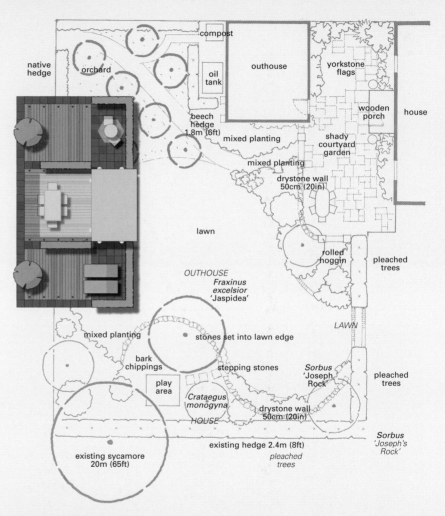

Style in a planting scheme
ABOVE These plans for a minimalist roof garden and a lush country garden show how the style of the garden will influence the planting.

Unity of mood or theme

Consider the mood or theme you are trying to create in the garden. Is it to be a woodland garden, a dry gravel Mediterranean one, or a garden for a young family? Each of these themes would require a very different approach to planting, which should enhance the strong sense of unity.

Unity of detail

You can create unity by restricting the palette of plants you choose. Use drifts of herbaceous and small plants. Duplicate plants, repeat forms and textures, and restrict the use of colour. There is always a great tendency to cram too many different plants into a design, thus creating a rather "dotty" effect. To ensure unity, reduce your plant selection early on, taking out half of the plants you have chosen and doubling up on those that are left.

Unity imposed by the site

Some sites will have such strong characteristics or "sense of place" that they impose a unity on the planting. A north-facing garden will be in permanent shade so only plants that tolerate those conditions can be selected. A rural site will suggest the range of native species around the boundaries, thereby blending garden and landscape together.

A sense of place
LEFT Here the existing oak woodland in plant expert Beth Chatto's garden, in Essex, UK, has imposed itself on the site and has resulted in the creation of a wonderful flourishing woodland garden.

Matching the mood
ABOVE In this coastal garden the foliage and flowers of the phormiums reflect the shapes of the sailing boats beyond.

The importance of simplicity

Simplicity can be defined as "less is more". It is all about showing constraint so that a garden or planting scheme does not become chaotic. In a small space simplicity means not jumbling up every possible colour form and texture together. In a larger space it entails visually separating different areas. Practically, simplicity means not putting all of your favourite plants into one planting scheme.

Harmony and contrast

In planting, the aim is to produce the right balance between harmony and contrast, and this is most successful when there is a suitable link between the plants. In the context of plants, harmony will exist between similar plant forms, textures, closely related colours, and direction of line – whether horizontal or vertical. Thus if you place plants with similar textures next to each other then you must ensure that either their forms or colours vary. If you position plants with similar forms beside each other then you must introduce a mixture of plant textures or colours.

Contrast is introduced to create interest and does not necessarily entail conflicting visual effects. For example, bergenia planted around a New Zealand flax (*Phormium tenax*) would show harmony of coarse texture but contrast of form, while a *Viburnum davidii* with a group of box (*Buxus sempervirens*) would reveal harmony of form (domes) but textural contrast.

Simplicity

ABOVE RIGHT Bold drifts of the same plant and the same colour provide a simple effect and help to draw you along the winding path. All will revert to green once flowering has finished.

Visual balance

BELOW RIGHT Draw a rough elevation so you can check that the heights and mass work together. You can then select appropriate plants to create the planned effect.

The importance of balance

It is the three-dimensional balance of the plant that you are considering – its height and mass – that is the important aspect of this topic. Balance is probably the hardest thing to get right, because plants tend to be quite small when they go into a planting scheme, and it is only as they mature that you can see if you have got the design right. You really need to draw a rough elevation as you select your plants in order to check the visual balance.

It is easiest to achieve balance in a formal planting design when each side of the design and planting is a mirror image of the other: for example, in a square lawn by positioning box spheres at each corner.

Most other types of planting scheme are reliant on asymmetrical balance, that is when a large plant such as a tree is visually matched by planting several smaller plants together on the other side. What is important is that the overall mass on each side echoes the other.

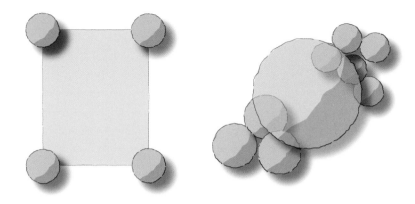

Achieving visual balance

ABOVE An identical plant at each corner in a symmetrical design (above left) creates the same effect as a greater number of small plants in an asymmetrical design (above right).

Symmetry

RIGHT Planting in which each side is a mirror image of the other has here created a strong sense of balance, reinforcing the axis of this path leading to the front door.

Asymmetry

FAR RIGHT Asymmetrical balance is achieved by planting three phormiums in a triangle equidistance apart.

Emphasis or focal-point planting

Some plants have exciting qualities and demand attention, because they have a special characteristic such as a strong form or habit or a coarse texture. A focal-point tree might have beautiful bark such as paper-bark maple (*Acer griseum*) or the birch *Betula utilis* var. *jacquemontii*, while a good focal-point shrub could be *Fatsia japonica* or *Euphorbia characias*.

It is important to select and place such accent plants with care, and they should be the first ones to be placed in the garden or planting scheme. Depending on the size and layout of the garden there may be only one focal-point plant – or there could be several sited around the garden. Make sure that only one can be seen at any one time otherwise the effect can become chaotic. Focal-point plants are also used to draw attention to an area of planting that could otherwise be just a green fuzz.

Scale and proportion

Scale refers to size, and you can only assess how large something is when you can compare its proportions to yourself and the surrounding landscape. When selecting plants you must think about: the size of the site (is it a small garden or a large park?); the size of the associated buildings (are they single or multistorey?); and the size of the actual area to be planted (is it a narrow

Accent plant
LEFT Paper-bark maple (*Acer griseum*) makes an ideal focal point because its cinnamon bark, pretty foliage, and autumn colour provide all-year interest.

Enduring interest
RIGHT By placing a pot in the front of this beautiful acer, the designer has ensured that the tree will continue as a focal point well into winter, when its tracery of branches is on show.

Repetition

LEFT The forms, textures, and colours of these grasses and sedges are repeated to great effect, producing a strong sense of unity with the building behind.

Out of balance

ABOVE In this garden entitled 'The Loire, Willows, and Silken Stone' at Château de Chaumont, in France, the shapes of the willow leaves are repeated in the panels and on the ground. The scale of the planting is too small, however, and the full effect is lost.

border or large open space?). You also need to consider the size of any other plants already on the site. The scale and proportion of planting can have an enormous influence on the mood of the garden. If plants are too large a space may become dark and claustrophobic, whereas if they are too small it may then feel open and exposed.

Repetition in the planting scheme

When planning your planting be sure to include a plant more than once. Sometimes unity can be reinforced by picking up on a plant – or a plant form or colour – that is outside the boundary, and using it in your planting. It may not be feasible to repeat a plant throughout the garden, but where you have sun and shade, for example, you could select a grass for the sunny area and a sedge for the shady one. This would provide repetition of form and texture, thus creating unity between the different areas.

All plants should work together to provide year-round interest as well as seasonal excitement. You therefore need to think about plants as design material. Every plant should fulfil a definite role within the planting scheme – whether it is to provide wonderful autumn colour or to enhance a certain viewpoint. Once you have decided on the roles that the planting will play, you can then start to select the plants that will best achieve these aims. This will involve analysing their individual characteristics, so that these can be combined so as to create a well-designed scheme.

2 plants in design

structure

For many people a two-dimensional garden plan starts to come alive only when they begin to think about the planting itself. By introducing height into the garden, plants establish the third dimension. They define the spaces and create enclosure as well as reinforcing the overall mood or style of the garden. It is all too easy at this stage to get carried away and choose all your favourite plants – those with beautiful flowers or colourful leaves. Restraint is needed.

In order for planting to be successful you need to think about the role that the various plants are playing within the overall design and planting scheme. If for example the garden is very overlooked, your first thoughts may be of how to provide some privacy and block out the offending buldings. If a rural garden is very exposed and windy, then selecting plants for a windbreak will be at the top of your priorities.

Planting can be broken down into distinct categories, depending on their roles – structural, focal point, ornamental, ground cover, and functional planting – and when selecting a plant you should note into which category it falls. For example, English oak (*Quercus robur*) would be structural; paper-bark maple (*Acer griseum*) focal point; *Verbena bonariensis* ornamental; *Bergenia cordifolia* ground cover; and a pear tree would be functional planting. In a small garden or urban street, however, the roles of the plants may be less clear, and a tree planted primarily as structure will usually have ornamental qualities such as flowers or autumn fruit as well.

Structural planting

It is structural planting that provides the ceilings and walls of gardens and landscapes, defining the spaces and creating enclosure. Structural planting should always be considered first, and trees and hedges should be named on the final plan, because these will influence the framework of the garden and the way you and your visitors move through it. Structural plants are the backbone of any planting scheme, and they need to be hardy, reliable, and relatively fast growing.

Many trees and shrubs that are used for structural planting in the landscape are European natives such as birch, ash, oak, hawthorn, and field maple. These are inexpensive because they are raised from seed, and they grow quickly, being well adapted to local soils and climate. The majority of European native trees and shrubs, however, are deciduous, but in the

Structural planting

RIGHT This planting category plays a very important role in gardens and the wider landscape. Structural plants such as trees are the backbone for other plants, and they also help to soften buildings and link them into their surroundings.

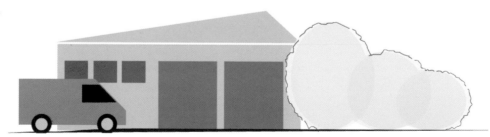

Trees and shrubs screening out large buildings.

Shrubs used to create privacy around buildings.

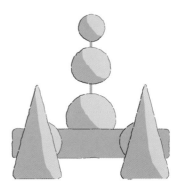

Defining the space
LEFT When shaped to form a hedge, *Elaeagnus* x *ebbingei* provides enclosure and outlines this area of hard landscaping.

Keep it simple
RIGHT AND BELOW Holly (*Ilex*) spheres form a strong focal point beyond the archway. The pyramids of box (*Buxus*) clutter the scene, competing with the spheres and distracting the eye from the main focal point.

garden you need structural plants that will provide an evergreen backdrop, so a broader range of plants is used. Other important qualities of structural plants include plain green leaves that are of fine or medium texture, and preferably evergreen (for shrubs). Structural plants should not demand attention. They also need to be readily available, so acquaint yourself with your local wholesale nursery catalogue and use this as your source.

Focal-point planting

Plants chosen as focal points should have a good year-round presence. Their role in the planting is to draw the eye, and they should be used with care. They need to have permanence; fleeting colour from flowers or autumn foliage is usually not enough. Accent plants should stand out from the plants around them, and this can be achieved by selecting one with a strong form or habit such as a fastigiate or weeping tree, a clipped form, coarse texture (for example, *Fatsia japonica*), or coloured bark or stems.

Ornamental planting

The most dynamic and exciting part of the planting is the ornamental plants, which provide daily and seasonal changes. This category may include trees, shrubs, herbaceous plants, grasses, bulbs, and annuals. Your selection will be influenced not only by your own likes and dislikes but also by the wide range of plant forms and textures, flower and foliage colour, coloured bark and stems, fruit or berries, and autumn foliage colour. Always consider what the plant will look like for the rest of the year when it is not performing. An example of a poor choice would be *Philadelphus* 'Belle Etoile' – a deciduous shrub that produces beautiful perfumed white flowers in late spring and early summer, but for the rest of the year it looks quite dull. Mexican orange blossom (*Choisya ternata*) would be a better choice, because this is evergreen, provides all-year structure, and flowers in late spring and again in late summer. Try not to base your plant selection purely on a picture in a plant encyclopedia. Instead, restrict yourself to those plants you know and have perhaps grown, even if this does at first seem a very limited palette of plants. Acquire a range of nursery catalogues so that you can source plants such as roses, herbaceous plants, and grasses that may be more difficult to find at a general wholesale nursery.

Good value
A hebe provides year-round interest because of its evergreen foliage and its flowers in summer through to autumn.

Textural variety
The silvery stems and soft lilac flowers of *Perovskia atriplicifolia* have a light airy texture from midsummer well into late autumn.

Ornamental variation
LEFT In Kilmokea garden in Ireland the flowers of the rhododendron and ceanothus create colour and excitement in late spring. These will soon fade, however, leaving the colourful foliage of the acer and hostas to last all summer.

Bold form
A standard bay tree gives height and a strong shape to the back of the border.

Useful structure
Evergreen *Choisya ternata* provides structure on the wall. It will usually flower in both spring and late summer, giving very good value to any planting scheme.

Colour harmony
A mid-border evergreen shrub such as *Euphorbia characias* has heavy heads of lime-green bracts in spring, and these combine well with late spring-flowering tulips.

Focal point
A clipped box sphere near the front of the border helps to prevent the planting from becoming a green fuzz.

Ground cover planting

Ground cover can easily be overlooked, but it plays an important role in any planting scheme. It creates the floors of outdoor spaces. The plants may be shrubs or herbaceous plants, and they ground the larger more exuberant plants. Many will form domes or hummocks: for example, cranesbill (*Geranium macrorrhizum*) and *Euonymus fortunei* 'Emerald Gaiety'. Having a good shape and interesting foliage are more important than flowers.

Functional planting

This type of planting can be less important because it refers to those plants that are grown for very specific purposes. This could include planting trees for shade or to provide timber or fruit. It could also be used for food-producing areas in the garden or to describe a tree that is wanted for the construction of a tree house.

Double act
ABOVE *Pachysandra terminalis* and a small-leaved variegated ivy combine well as ground cover to soften the edge of the hard landscaping.

Functional plant choice
ABOVE In his own garden in Belgium, gardening designer Jacques Wirtz has used undulating box hedging as ground cover to unite lawn and hard landscaping.

trees

All around you in rural and urban environments are trees, yet they are very often taken for granted until their existence is perhaps threatened by a new housing development. It is always amazing how few people even notice the trees in their own street or local park, and certainly cannot identify them. If you are going to be involved in the selection of trees for your garden then you do need to acquire some knowledge, as a tree will take many years to reach its full potential, and planting the wrong one can cause all sorts of problems in the future. Trees are continually interacting with their environment, and many factors influence their growth and size. These include the local and regional climate: rain, wind, aspect, frost, and length of growing season. The soil will have a huge influence on growth rate, as will competition from neighbours. Damage done by pests and diseases, and human pressures such as pollution and vandalism will all affect the establishment and growth of any tree.

Tree selection

Trees should always be the starting point in your planting design, so you should go through a thorough process before making your choice. Have a good tree book to hand, and if you are unsure about your ideas ask a reliable tree nursery for advice. Considerations about the site are covered in more detail in the plant selection chapter (see pp.82–105).

Before deciding on a particular tree, consider its role within the planting scheme. Is it providing structure, is its role purely ornamental, or is it being used to create a focal point? This will then help you to define the visual characteristics you require. It is also important to understand the atmosphere or style that a particular tree will create. Silver birch (*Betula pendula*) for example could create a natural woodland atmosphere, while catalpa or eucalyptus are more sculptural and would therefore enhance the style of a modern garden.

Structural planting

You will be using trees as structure if you want to create a woodland or wildlife habitat, provide avenue or street planting, establish shelter on an exposed site, screen out poor views, form boundaries, or give privacy. Trees used for structural planting make up the framework of any design. Therefore they should be reliable varieties that fit naturally into the landscape, even though they may not be natives; they must establish quickly in the given soil and site conditions. Choose trees with fine or medium texture and plain green leaves. No brightly coloured foliage should ever be used for structural planting.

Effective forms

RIGHT AND FAR RIGHT Olive trees (right) and fastigiate hornbeams (far right) are used to provide height and structure in these small gardens. They also define the shape of the space, and their forms will give them a strong winter presence.

Rhythm and repetition

LEFT The white trunks of these birch trees are providing structural interest at ground level and are also reinforcing the architecture – the white walls and the white pavilion in the background.

Trees can be used as screen planting both in the garden and the landscape. In the garden you may plant a tree or group of trees to help hide adjacent buildings and create privacy for the users. Evergreen trees are obviously best for this, but many such as leyland cypress are far too large and their inappropriate use has created enormous problems over the years.

Where space is limited, a row of pleached trees may be appropriate. Pleached trees are like a hedge on legs and they are used extensively in Europe to provide shade in city streets and also to separate and screen houses from busy roads. The most popular trees for pleaching are hornbeam and lime, because they are quick growing. *Pyrus calleryana* 'Chanticleer' – a cultivar of the Chinese wild pear with glossy leaves and rich autumn colour – makes a lovely pleached hedge in a garden. To create a pleached hedge the trees are grown to about 1.8m (6ft) before their leaders are cut off, and their branches are trained sideways on canes or wires to make an avenue.

Where space is limited, you can also use fastigiate trees as structural planting: for example, the apple *Malus tschonoskii* and fastigiate hornbeams (*Carpinus*) are often seen as street trees in towns and cities.

To produce shelter, trees can be very effective, although shelterbelts occupy a considerable amount of space so can be planted only where room allows. For a tall hedge you could use a single row of conifers or plant evergreen holm oak (*Quercus ilex*), which provides very effective shelter near the coast, because it is tolerant of sea spray.

Ornamental planting

Choosing ornamental trees should be exciting, and in many smaller spaces such as gardens, courtyards, urban streets, and squares you may find that the role of ornamental planting merges with that of structural planting. Ornamental trees are usually planted in beds or borders, so the tree canopy should be relatively light, allowing shrubs and herbaceous plants to grow happily beneath.

You should consider each tree's particular visual characteristics as well as how it can help to reinforce the style or mood of the overall design and planting. In a rural garden you will probably choose natives around the boundaries so that the garden fuses with the landscape beyond. You could then introduce cultivars of natives or species as you move away from the boundaries. Strong foliage colours such as purple and gold should be avoided in any rural landscape, where they always look out of place. Concentrate instead on foliage texture – the very fine texture of Japanese

pagoda tree (*Sophora japonica*) will create a strong form, while the coarse one of Indian bean tree (*Catalpa bignonioides*) will attract attention.

Your choice of tree should complement the other plants with its seasonal interest and colour, and in a small garden it should have more than one season of interest: *Amelanchier lamarckii*, for example, has spring flowers and good autumn colour. Birds also enjoy its small black fruits. In summer, when many shrubs and herbaceous plants are at their best, trees can be used to provide foliage colour or simply to create shade and provide structure.

It should be possible to include at least one tree for autumn interest in even the smallest garden. For maximum effect, position trees, shrubs, and other plants for autumn interest close together, because the reds and golds of foliage and berries can look wonderful with the blue, purple, and golden flowers of autumn. Place trees chosen for winter interest where they will catch the winter sun and close to a path if possible, so that you can touch the bark as you pass. Underplant spring-flowering trees with bulbs.

Many functions
LEFT In this garden the white mulberry (*Morus alba*) in the centre is fulfilling more than one role. It is extremely ornamental, and its bright green colour and relatively coarse foliage will ensure that it gives a long season of interest. The tree is also providing shade in this small space, as can be seen from the shadows on the ground.

Seasonal interest
RIGHT These ornamental trees have a wide range of roles in the garden.
1 *Cercis siliquastrum* for spring flowers
2 *Gleditsia triacanthos* 'Sunburst' for golden foliage
3 Small evergreen pine for form and texture all year
4 *Amelanchier lamarckii* for spring flowers and autumn colour
5 *Acer griseum* for peeling bark
6 *Sorbus vilmorinii* for autumn berries
7 Many spring-flowering *Prunus* also for autumn colour
8 *Betula pendula* for interesting bark
9 *Liquidambar styraciflua* for vivid autumn colour

TREES AS FOCAL POINTS

Choose a tree that will be of interest for as long as possible during the year. In a large garden this might be cedar of Lebanon (*Cedrus libani*) or the oak *Quercus robur* 'Fastigiata', which have strong habits and forms. In a smaller garden your choice is more restricted and would depend on the site conditions. One possibility might be Japanese maple, for attractive foliage in summer and a strong sculptural form in winter. Consider how you could reinforce the presence of the tree by underplanting with spring bulbs or by placing a seat or piece of sculpture at its base.

Most acers have more than one season of interest so they can work well as a focal point.

shrubs

Over the past few years, shrubs seem to have become less popular, with gardeners preferring "naturalistic" planting schemes of herbaceous plants and grasses rather than mixed borders. If your garden is shady, however, and you struggle with heavy clay, then you will know that herbaceous plants will not thrive in these conditions and you will welcome the structure, year-round presence, and green backdrop provided by shrubs. You can quickly learn how to manipulate these plants so that with a certain amount of strategic pruning you can turn them from lumpy domes into elegant clean-stemmed plants or well-clipped wall shrubs.

Shrubs can offer so much more throughout the year than the ephemeral plantings of herbaceous plants and grasses, particularly in small spaces.

Providing the soil and aspect are suitable, a wide range of hardy woody plants from around the world – such as *Pittosporum tenuifolium* from New Zealand and French lavender (*Lavandula stoechas*) – can be grown in a temperate climate, even though most native shrubs such as *Viburnum opulus* or English holly (*Ilex aquifolium*) are not widely used in gardens.

When selecting shrubs for a planting scheme, you need to go through the same process as for a tree (see p.44), checking the site and the visual characteristics of the plant before making your decisions. Shrubs fall into several categories depending on the role they play in the design: they can be structural, focal-point plants, ornamental or ground cover.

Structural planting

Structural shrubs provide the framework for all the other planting. When creating a planting scheme select these shrubs first. The most useful ones are evergreen, and they need to be hardy, reliable, and relatively fast growing so that they establish quickly, are easy to find, and are inexpensive. As opposed to the limited range of evergreen trees, there is a wide variety of evergreen shrubs available. Those used for structural planting should have fine or medium texture and plain green leaves. Your choice of structural shrubs may well include Portugal laurel (*Prunus lusitanica*), *Elaeagnus* x *ebbingei*, *Osmanthus* x *burkwoodii,* and strawberry tree (*Arbutus unedo*).

Tall structural planting can be used to screen unsightly features such as a car park, refuse bin, or oil tank. To be effective, the planting needs to be taller than eye level, that is, more than 1.5m (5ft) high. Always use plants

Clever pruning
LEFT An avenue of *Viburnum rhytidophyllum* gives structure to this garden. The shrubs have been elegantly cut so that the bare sculptural stems allow a view down the garden and planting to be established around them.

Structural planting below eye height

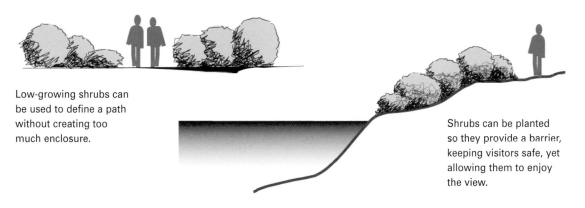

Low-growing shrubs can be used to define a path without creating too much enclosure.

Shrubs can be planted so they provide a barrier, keeping visitors safe, yet allowing them to enjoy the view.

The outdoor room
ABOVE Shrubs effectively screen this sitting area so that it feels private and is a pleasant place to relax.

with small green leaves for screening so that they do not in any way attract attention. Avoid variegated, coarse texture, or coloured leaves when trying to hide an object. Fine- or medium-textured climbers on a trellis could also be used for screening. Similarly, a sitting area may be screened from neighbours by planting tall shrubs so they are close to one another.

In an urban garden you usually need to obscure the fences with structural shrubs at the back of any planting, and in a rural landscape natives or cultivars of natives can be used to define the boundaries. A large garden can include structural shrubs instead of walls or fences, to define separate areas.

Planting around an outbuilding will help to anchor and soften its impact while connecting it to the surrounding area. Shrubs can also be used to create privacy, because it keeps people away from the building.

Introduce structural planting in a border to provide a backdrop for the other plants. Where space allows this could be a yew hedge, while in a smaller space it will usually involve a range of structural shrubs. In a mixed border you will need some smaller evergreen shrubs to create structure and provide a winter presence in its centre. Shrubs such as sarcococca, box (*Buxus*), hebes, small skimmias, lavenders, and *Viburnum davidii* are very useful in this role.

Shrubs that are above knee height but below eye height (0.6–1.5m/2–5ft) can also have a structural role in planting design. Plants this high will limit access without obstructing views, while structural planting about 1m (3ft) high can provide a barrier in front of water, vehicles, or a steep slope, yet allows you to see the view beyond.

For shelter from cold winds, a hedge or a mixed planting of shrubs might be appropriate. Fast-growing natives and their cultivars are most tolerant of cold winds, so plants such as hawthorn, holly, field maple, or hornbeam are suitable in exposed rural areas.

It is very important when designing that your possible movements and those of your visitors through and around the garden are noted so that the natural desire lines can be followed. If you ignore these lines, garden users will establish their own quick routes through the planting, which then becomes trampled under foot. To keep people on a particular path or route, use low structural planting to emphasize and reinforce the direction.

In a front garden ensure that any structural planting that is adjacent to the driveway is kept low, so that it does not restrict the view of oncoming traffic for drivers leaving the property.

Shrubs as ornamental planting

Here you really are spoilt for choice. So many shrubs are available that making a decision can be extremely difficult. Selection, however, must be dictated by the site and the soil, the style and theme of the planting, and your own preferences. Colour too can play an important part in the refinement process.

Ornamental shrubs can provide: coloured foliage; spring, summer, autumn, or winter flowers; autumn-coloured foliage, fruits, and berries; and coloured stems. In a small garden one season of interest such as summer flowers may not be enough; shrubs should have a strong form, eye-catching texture, or coloured foliage as well, so that they look attractive when their lovely flowers have long been forgotten. For example, when selecting a weigela or philadelphus – both of which flower for a short time in late spring – find cultivars that have coloured or variegated foliage so that the season of interest extends into late summer.

When choosing plants for different seasons it is generally more successful to group together plants that share the same season of interest rather than

Shrubs as focal points

You should always introduce some "specials" into your planting scheme. These need to be placed with care, because they provide the punctuation marks in the planting. Depending on the layout and size of your garden, you may have one major special or several spaced out around it. Remember though that too many exciting plants will make a space seem restless.

Any shrub chosen as a focal point must possess some architectural or sculptural quality. This could be a strong form (for example, a clipped box sphere or a spiky phormium), a distinctive habit (for example, *Viburnum plicatum* 'Mariesii'), or very bold foliage (for example, *Fatsia japonica*). To be really successful, a focal point needs to have year-round presence. Such plants must fit in with the overall style and theme of the planting, and you need to select them very early on in the planning process so that their strong outline appears on your initial rough elevation.

Effectively shaped forms
ABOVE LEFT Clipped box (*Buxus*) spheres and cones establish points of interest and provide height within the low box hedges. Too many strong shapes within a small area are, however, distracting.

A real performer
RIGHT *Viburnum plicatum* 'Mariesii' has a strong horizontal habit and produces a wonderful display of flowers in late spring, making it a very "good value" plant in the garden.

dotting them around the garden. This seasonal support may be provided by ground cover, herbaceous plants, or bulbs: for example, *Hamamelis mollis*, which flowers in midwinter and enjoys a shady position, could be planted with sarcococcas, hellebores, and seasonal bulbs such as snowdrops to make a delightful winter grouping.

Shrubs as ground cover

Ground cover plants play an important role in any planting scheme. They help conserve moisture, smother weeds so reducing maintenance, add interest to a planting design at ground level, soften the edges of a border, create a link with the hard landscape, and anchor the larger shrubs and other plants.

The main characteristic of ground cover is that plants should grow out and successfully cover the surrounding soil; fortunately, a wide range of plants fulfil this requirement. Evergreen plants are best because they provide year-round cover. For similar reasons you should select plants for their good form or interesting foliage rather than for their flowers. Where space is limited, opt for compact well-behaved shrubs such as *Euonymus fortunei* 'Emerald Gaiety'; and where a large area needs to be covered quickly plant rampant spreaders such as the honeysuckle *Lonicera pileata* and rose of Sharon (*Hypericum calycinum*).

In an extensive area, plant larger shrubs at very close spacing to encourage dense cover. The size of these plants is then controlled by close and regular trimming with a hedge cutter. Insert a few architectural plants such as *Mahonia japonica* to provide interest above the ground cover. Such schemes are effective at controlling movement around the garden, and if mainly evergreens are used there is the bonus of year-round interest.

Winter wonders
ABOVE RIGHT The beautifully coloured stems of cornus and willows standing alongside this lake have been planted so that they catch the winter sunshine.

Suitable ground cover
BELOW RIGHT In this natural woodland ivy provides effective year-round ground cover under the trees.

hedges and windbreaks

A hedge may quite simply be described as some shrubs planted close together in a row. Once the plants have merged, they provide a solid green living structure.

Hedges are generally considered as structural planting, and you should identify the hedge and state its height on your plan, because both pieces of information will influence the mood and style of the garden. Hedges can be used: for boundaries; to divide up internal spaces; as a backdrop for other planting; to reinforce walkways and paths; to provide shelter from cold winds; as a habitat for wildlife; and to create herb and knot gardens.

Formal hedges

A formal hedge is trimmed regularly to its defined shape. It needs to have fine texture (that is, small leaves) so that it can be maintained with a hedge trimmer, and it must have a twiggy structure and respond well to regular cutting. Tall evergreen hedges (1.5–1.8m/5–6ft) should be cut with a batter, that is, they should be wider at the base than the top. This allows light to reach the lower part of the hedge and also makes the hedge more stable.

The very best formal hedge is yew, which is fine textured, dark leaved, and non-reflective. This makes it the ideal backdrop for herbaceous plants and more ornamental planting. Yew can be shaped in a variety of ways, such as a wavy hedge, pillar, or swirl, to introduce structure into modern herbaceous planting schemes. Beech, although deciduous, also makes an excellent formal hedge; when trimmed, it keeps its juvenile characteristic of retaining the dead brown leaves during winter. It makes a particularly good hedge if planted in a double row, allowing 30cm (12in) between plants and 45cm (18in) between rows. For a low formal hedge under 30cm (12in) high the box *Buxus sempervirens* 'Suffruticosa' is excellent.

Formal hedges must be accessible for clipping, so allow for this when planning your garden or border. Also, when planted as a boundary, it should be borne in mind that the regular maintenance required on formal hedges creates work for the next door neighbour, too; a border of mixed shrubs would need less work. Because hedges absorb water and nutrients from the soil, they may not be a good choice if the soil is dry or the border is very narrow.

Adaptable hedging

LEFT Hedges can be established using a great variety of different plants, in all manner of forms – from soft and curvy to crisp and architectural.

1 Beech is good for strong architectural forms over and alongside a path
2 The dark structure of the hedge provides a dramatic background for soft silvers and blues
3 Box hedging creates the structure for a loosely planted knot garden
4 Hedging is suitable for the walls and supporting buttresses of an outdoor room
5 Hedging can be used instead of a brick wall alongside steps
6 These wonderful soft lumpy hedges are now a trademark of the Belgian landscape-architect Jacques Wirtz
7 A beech arch frames a vista beyond, and architectural shapes reinforce the route
8 An arch and clipped cones of box direct the eye to the focal point beyond
9 A flowering hedge of escallonia offers a soft division between other ornamentals
10 Strong forms of shaped yew create architectural topiary

Formal hedges

RIGHT Clipped hedges add strong form and rhythm to any planting scheme. Short hedges under 1m (3ft) high, of the honeysuckle *Lonicera nitida* for example, should have straight sides and top, while taller hedges should be cut with a very slight inward slope, or batter, at the sides.

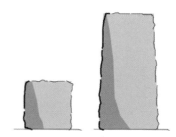

Informal hedges

An informal hedge tends to be more ornamental than a formal one and is chosen for its flowers, foliage, or fruit. It can be deciduous (for example, the cherry *Prunus cerasifera* 'Nigra') or evergreen (*Viburnum tinus*). It is usually only clipped to keep it at a suitable size and to create a more natural shape. Secateurs rather than a hedge cutter are used for this task.

Informal hedges are good as boundaries or for internal division. In rural areas such hedges are often used to create field boundaries, and comprise a mix of native plants such as hawthorn, field maple, hazel, dog rose, blackthorn, holly, and cornus. These plants can be bought bare-root from specialist nurseries, and because they are raised from seed a mixed hedge is relatively inexpensive to plant. Hedges are also useful wildlife habitats.

Country hedgerow

BELOW This rural hedge, which is composed of a mixture of native plants, will be a source of seasonal interest for its flowers, autumn colour, and fruit as well as a habitat for insects, birds, and small mammals.

Greenery in the city

TOP An informal hedge of *Photinia* x *fraseri* creates shelter and privacy around this urban roof garden.

Informal boundary

ABOVE A hedge of native beech provides an attractive demarcation between this garden and the adjacent field.

Hedge windows
ABOVE Openings have been created in this hornbeam hedge so that views of the woodland beyond can be enjoyed.

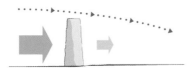

Providing protection
ABOVE AND BELOW A hedge that is 1.8m (6ft) high will give good shelter for up to 18m (60ft) on the leeward side.

Windbreaks

Wind can cause many problems in a garden, and therefore you should erect some sort of windbreak. The reasons for this are:

- the soil will warm up more quickly and cool down more slowly, so giving a longer growing season than normal and allowing a greater variety of plants to be grown.
- buds will not be desiccated so there will be increased plant growth and less structural damage to plants.
- less soil erosion and less evaporation.
- a pleasanter environment in which to work or relax.

Although wind can be reduced by erecting a solid barrier such as a wall, this will also cause eddies and turbulence on either side. A semi-permeable barrier such as a hedge will be far more beneficial. The plants must be hardy and able to withstand cold winds; therefore native species are often best. However, native evergreen yew and holly are quite slow growing, so often conifers such as lawson cypress (*Chamaecyparis lawsoniana*), leyland cypress (X *Cupressocyparis leylandii*), and western red cedar (*Thuja plicata*) are used.

The effectiveness of a windbreak is determined by its height and width. Maximum benefit occurs up to a distance of ten times the height of hedge or other windbreak. The whole sheltered zone may extend to 30 times the height of the windbreak, that is 54m (180ft). The ratio of width to height is also important, because if the hedge is not wide enough the wind will be deflected around each end, leading to increased wind speed at certain points in the garden. The ratio should be 12:1. Therefore, if the hedge is 1.8m (6ft) high, its width should be 21.6m (70ft). These are very useful calculations to remember and also apply to larger shelterbelts where you are planting trees and shrubs.

PLEACHED HEDGES

The Romans were the first to introduce pleached hedges, that is hedges on "stilts". They can provide a very quick way of introducing screening into a garden because they can be bought "ready made". Beech, hornbeam, lime, and pear are the most frequently used plants. Their clear stems are normally about 1.8m (6ft) high, and the branches of each tree will span sideways for about 3m (10ft) in total. You will need to provide a framework of wire supports for the branches until they are mature and well established.

These wooden frames, supporting the newly planted pleached trees, will eventually be replaced with a framework of wires.

Plant selection

When selecting a wall shrub or climbing plant do think carefully about the space available and ensure that the height, width, and strength of the wall or other structure will be suitable for the chosen plant. Many of these plants are extremely vigorous and will quickly outgrow their allotted space. Frequent pruning often means that the natural form of the plant is destroyed, and it is not able to flower or fruit as it should. Boston ivy (*Parthenocissus tricuspidata*) is a prime example of a climber that is sometimes planted against a house wall, yet it can quickly reach 12m (40ft) or more, and so may cause problems.

Also consider the aspect of the structure against which the plant is to be grown. When selecting wall shrubs and climbers it is simplest to think of those plants that are tolerant of a north- or east-facing wall in one category and those that need the warmth and shelter of a south- or west-facing wall in another. Although temperate winters are becoming warmer and there are fewer frosts, avoid planting camellias or Mexican orange blossom (*Choisya ternata*) on an east-facing wall, because the early morning sun on frosted flowers or foliage causes considerable damage. On a south- or west-facing wall grow plants such as *Clematis armandii* or pineapple broom (*Cytisus battandieri*), which will really benefit from its microclimate and could not be grown elsewhere in the garden.

Climbers and wall shrubs can do structural damage to brickwork, pipes, drains, or roof tiles, or cause damp patches, so ensure that this will not be a problem in your garden and that everything is in good condition. If you are wanting to plant at the base of a wall, check the site before buying the plants. Make sure that the footings allow enough space for planting and that any roof overhang does not make the soil too dry.

Plants used on pergolas or beams need to grow tall to reach the top of the posts and cover the crossbeams. Pendulous flowers such as wisteria and laburnum are very suitable, because they will be readily noticed. Avoid overplanting a pergola on overhead beams so the space beneath does not become dark and tunnel-like.

When making your selection it is also very important to consider the amount of maintenance the plant will require and the level of skill needed to prune it. You will not be pleased if you plant a rambler on a pergola or a wisteria on your house wall and then do not have the time or the skill to cope with it. No wall shrubs or climbing plants are maintenance free, but some are much easier to manage than others. They can harbour pests and diseases such as snails and mildew, so should be checked regularly.

Plants on a pergola
ABOVE This pergola has been planted with vines creating a feeling of enclosure while still allowing dappled sunshine into the space.

Give plants room
RIGHT *Hydrangea anomala* subsp. *petiolaris* can quickly outgrow its allotted space, so it needs to be grown on a large wall or up into a tree.

Wooden supports
FAR RIGHT Trellis panels and arches must be strong if they are to hold up such an exuberant climbing rose.

Supports for climbers and wall shrubs

At the same time as you make your plant selection, think about the method of support that will be required. This must be in good condition and able to take the weight of the fully developed plant, which can be quite considerable after heavy rain or in strong wind. Remember that the support may be on view for some time until the plant becomes established, so it needs to be relatively attractive or unobtrusive.

The most popular form of support for plants trained on walls is a system of vine eyes and galvanized wires. As it develops, the plant is tied onto the wires. A similar system using screw-threaded vine eyes can also be used on fences. All manner of decorative trellis panels in timber or metal can be mounted onto walls or fences to provide support. The panel should be mounted onto battens, so that there is room for air to circulate behind the panels. This reduces the risk of fungal diseases such as mildew, which can be a real problem, especially on climbing roses. When tying in wall plants use a material – such as soft string or raffia – that will decompose naturally, so that it does not damage or restrict the growth of stems in future years.

PLANTING TECHNIQUES

Prepare a planting hole 30cm (12in) away from the support. Do this well because often the soil will be poor and dry at the base of a structure such as a wall. To help retain moisture, add a good quantity of well-rotted organic matter in the base and work it in. (Note that clematis should be planted in a deep hole with the rootball at least 10cm (4in) below soil level, because this will help to prevent clematis wilt.) Place the climber or wall shrub in the hole, angling it towards the support and leaving its original support cane in place. Mulch the plant and keep it well watered during its first growing season. As the plant develops, tie it into trellis fixed 5cm (2in) off the wall.

Fremontodendron californicum

herbaceous plants

It is herbaceous plants that provide the real seasonal excitement and colour in your garden, and they are available today in a seemingly endless array of old and new cultivars. The definition of an herbaceous perennial has changed over the years. Traditionally they were described as a plant that comes up every year, produces stems that become slightly woody, and then dies back in late autumn. The dead stems and seedheads were then cut back, and the plants survived underground during winter. Nowadays the term herbaceous perennial tends to include evergreen plants such as bergenias, hellebores, and heucheras, and many of the "new" herbaceous plants and cultivars produce interesting seed and dried flower heads that are left to stand over the winter months before being cut down in early spring.

The use of herbaceous plants has also varied over the years. The traditional herbaceous border that was popularized by such gardeners as Gertrude Jekyll has largely given way to the mixed border and the naturalistic and prairie styles of planting made popular by Piet Oudolf in Holland and by Wolfgang Oehme and James van Sweden in America.

The traditional herbaceous border

Such a border is backed by a tall formal hedge, such as yew, or a wall, so providing shelter and a backdrop for the planting. It should be about 3m (10ft) deep and have a ratio of at least 4:1 length to depth. Borders are viewed from the front or along their length and frequently have a corridor of grass between them. The planting needs to be in bold drifts with the taller plants at the back, and great thought must be given to the forms and colours of the flowers. Inspiring herbaceous borders can be seen at Arley Hall in Cheshire, UK, and Newby Hall in North Yorkshire, UK.

The borders are usually designed to be at their most beautiful between early and late summer, and they may have a strong colour theme. Lilies and cannas are sometimes planted out in pots to fill gaps left by early-flowering plants such as paeonies or poppies. Such traditional herbaceous borders are very heavy on preparation and maintenance, because the soil needs to be deeply cultivated, the tall plants at the back require staking, and all the plants need regular deadheading to maintain their performance. The plants should also be lifted and divided every five years to regenerate them.

The mixed border

As gardens have become smaller and labour more expensive so the style of gardens and planting has changed. Small plots in towns and cities are generally surrounded by fences or some form of boundary, and herbaceous

plants alone do not offer any structure or year-round interest, nor do they screen out these boundaries. The mixed border is now probably the most successful style of planting seen in gardens today. In such a border, shrubs provide all-year structure and screening, while a range of herbaceous plants produce seasonal excitement and bulbs extend the floral interest. A mixed border requires far less maintenance than an herbaceous one, and if herbaceous plants that need little or no staking are selected then the only regular maintenance during summer is deadheading and some cutting back.

At the back of the border interplant evergreen structural shrubs with tall herbaceous plants that have strong flower forms such as achilleas, aconitums, veronicastrums, and phlomis. Plants in the middle of the border should be exciting, and selected for their flower form and colour and for as long a season of flowering as possible. This group could include astrantias,

eryngiums, salvias, poppies, paeonies, penstemons, and hemerocallis. Low-growing herbaceous plants – some of which should be evergreen – are used at the front of the border to provide ground cover and a grounding for the taller herbaceous plants and shrubs. Hardy geraniums are wonderful in this role. Useful evergreen herbaceous plants are fringe cups (*Tellima grandiflora*), heucheras, bergenias, and epimediums.

Some herbaceous plants can be used to provide a link between the front and back of the border, and these are the ones that have a net-curtain-like quality: for example, *Verbena bonariensis*, purple fennel (*Foeniculum vulgare* 'Purpureum'), *Actaea simplex* cultivars, and sanguisorbas. John Brookes' garden, Denmans, in West Sussex, UK, provides a wonderful range of beds and borders containing a great variety of trees, shrubs, herbaceous plants, and bulbs that demonstrate this mixed style of planting.

Traditional border

LEFT The path between a traditional double herbaceous border allows low-growing plants at the front to flop over and soften the otherwise hard edge. The tall plants such as delphiniums at the back will require staking.

Small-scale border

RIGHT Here a low wall provides the backdrop for an herbaceous border that has been designed to fit beautifully into a small garden.

Naturalistic or new-wave perennial planting

The most recent approach to the use of herbaceous plants has been that based on ecological planting, that is "right plant, right place". This has resulted in planting compositions that are imaginative and relaxed in style while at the same time based on sound ecological principles. They can best be described as an "exotic meadow", where "exotic" means non-native rather than its more usual meaning of dramatic and colourful planting.

These ideas first came from Germany and were largely the result of the work of Richard Hansen – a gardener and scientist whose aim was to create beautiful gardens by harmonizing the artistic ideal with nature and plant habitat requirements. An excellent example of the planting style he pioneered is to be found in Westpark, a public park in Munich. Here there are exuberant drifts of naturalized perennials and grasses, which flower and peak in rich succession. The plant groups overlap and intermingle, and each plant has an important role to play, even when not in flower. The dominant plants are the tall grasses such as *Miscanthus sinensis*, and giant feather grass

Naturalistic planting

RIGHT Herbaceous plants and grasses have been used in loose drifts, with some taller plants near the front of the border. Many of the plants develop bold seedheads, and these are left standing to provide interest during winter.

Late-season interest

LEFT Even in autumn the naturalistic planting in Westpark, Munich, Germany, has a rich variety of forms and textures from the seedheads of herbaceous plants and grasses.

(*Stipa gigantea*) is often chosen as a single specimen. There then follow plants that naturally form groups, such as daylilies, asters, iris, and sedums. Finally ground-covering species, such as thyme and alchemilla, are used, and these form the carpet through which the taller plants grow.

The herbaceous plants that are selected must not only be well suited to the growing conditions but should also produce interesting seed and flower heads that survive well into winter, sparkling with frost and snow. They are cut down when no longer attractive. A wide range of grasses provide interesting contrasts of form and texture. In mild wet winters, however, the seed and flower heads will become wet and bedraggled well before the start of the new growing season.

When using plants in this more naturalistic way it is important that the ground preparation is very rigorous and that all perennial weeds are removed. If necessary the soil structure should be improved by the addition of organic matter. Avoid using fertilizers, because plants perform best if grown "hungry" and the addition of nitrogen fertilizers will just encourage lax vegetative growth at the expense of sturdy stems and flowers.

Beth Chatto has also been an advocate of the naturalistic style of ecological planting. Each area of her garden at Elmstead Market, in the UK, is given over to a particular habitat where she grows only the species that will flourish in those growing conditions. She has created her now-famous gravel and woodland gardens, damp and dry borders, and a Mediterranean garden. She uses trees and shrubs to provide height and structure in each of the areas and then selects her herbaceous plants for their form, texture, and colour. She accompanies the scientific approach with an artistic eye – a combination that produces planting that is strong, confident, informal, rhythmic, and uncontrived and sustains interest throughout the seasons with textural seedheads and dried flower heads.

In Holland the naturalistic style of planting has been explored and developed by Piet Oudolf. This landscape designer has set up his own nursery and produced a wide range of exciting perennials and cultivars that he uses in his planting schemes. He is always searching for improved hardiness, longer flowering periods, or improved flower colour. Oudolf's dramatic and beautiful plantings are frequently enclosed within a structural framework of sculptured or clipped yew and box hedges, creating a balance of formal and informal planting. Oudolf has also worked extensively in England, and you can see his planting schemes at the RHS gardens at Wisley, at Pensthorpe Wildfowl Trust in Norfolk, and at Scampston Hall in North Yorkshire.

All naturalistic plantings do best on light soil. On heavy clay soils the plants grow too tall and lax, and tend to flop over. Any plant that threatens to dominate a group either by spreading too vigorously or producing copious amounts of seed needs to be removed before it becomes a nuisance.

In the wide open spaces of America the landscape team of Oehme & van Sweden has developed "prairie-style" planting, which uses bold drifts of herbaceous plants and grasses. It, too, includes plants, such as rudbeckias, sedums, eupatoriums, and miscanthus, that produce interesting dried flower heads and seedheads and still retain form, texture, and colour over

the winter months. Designs and planting schemes by Oehme & van Sweden have transformed both public and private spaces in North America. Their naturalistic style of planting does require space, and while many of the herbaceous plants and grasses are suitable for small town gardens the need for some shrubs and a framework of structural planting as well does limit its adoption. The herbaceous plants in these schemes also require light open conditions, and often small gardens are subject to shade cast by house walls and boundaries, making many gardens unsuitable.

Woodland and woodland-edge gardens
Some herbaceous plants are ideal for shady areas under trees. In a small garden this may be under a single tree or a group of trees, and in some small town gardens the shade may be created by a house wall. When selecting plants you must differentiate between moist and dry shade – particularly as dry shade is the hardest of any situation in which to plant successfully.

Woodland planting

ABOVE Shade-loving herbaceous plants that will flower early in the year before the tree canopy emerges have here been combined with ferns and shrubs to create a delightful garden.

Sculptured hedges as backdrop

FAR LEFT Clipped yew hedges provide the structure and background for the naturalistic planting to be found in garden designer Piet Oudolf's own garden in The Netherlands.

Loose drifts

LEFT Tall herbaceous plants and grasses such as giant feather grass (*Stipa gigantea*) look wonderful on either side of the path at Bury Court, in Surrey, UK.

Most woodland plants flower early in the year before the tree canopy is fully out, so you should select plants that have interesting foliage and flowers otherwise the area will look very dull later on. Because newly planted trees provide little shade, plants that are tolerant of both sun and shade should be planted initially; once the shade canopy is established, true woodland perennials such as epimediums, asarum, and false solomon's seal (*Maianthemum racemosum*) can be grown. In an established woodland check out the fibrous roots of the trees; if there is a dense mat of roots it may be impossible to establish herbaceous perennials. Perennial plantings develop poorly under false acacias, birches, poplars, willows, and cherries.

Herbaceous plants are an amazingly versatile group of plants and can be used successfully in many different types of garden and planting scheme. Traditional plants such as delphiniums, lupins, paeonies, and poppies can be combined with more recent introductions such as *Knautia macedonica* and *Verbena bonariensis* to create a contemporary version of cottage-garden planting. Plants – such as ligularias, rodgersias, and astilbes – that are tolerant of very moist conditions are good for waterside and bog garden planting, too. Where space allows, borders can also be designed specifically to produce flowers for cutting and drying.

PLANT SELECTION

It is extremely important that all chosen plants thrive in the particular growing conditions of the site to which they have been designated and that they reflect the style and mood of the garden. Therefore you should think about how the plants are to be used – whether in a traditional or mixed border, or a more naturalistic style of planting. Once you have settled on this, study the characteristics of each plant. Flower form and colour are the most essential features for the tall and medium-sized plants that will be at the back and middle of the border. Are the flowers in a spike, button, daisy etc (see pp.14–15)? You also need to consider the overall height, and whether the plant will require staking. The texture and colour of the foliage will be important for those plants at the front of the border and for those with a short flowering season. Research the length of the flowering season, too. Is this species or cultivar giving the best value, or could it be exchanged for a better performer? Other considerations are rate of spread – how quickly will the plant fill its allotted space, and is it likely to become invasive? – and its hardiness. Once you have noted all these qualities, then you can start planning your planting scheme.

grasses

Grasses have enjoyed a great resurgence of interest over the last few years, and this has coincided with the popularity of the naturalistic style of planting using herbaceous plants and grasses. The strongly linear forms and fine texture of most grasses contrast very effectively with the bold foliage or distinctive flower forms of herbaceous perennials. Most grasses have fine-textured foliage. Their leaves may be soft and curvy or strongly vertical, and their flower heads are feathery, graceful, and diaphanous, bringing a light airy feel to the planting scheme. The flowers of the taller grasses move gently in the breeze and give a vertical lift that is refreshingly different from other plants.

Some grasses such as *Anemanthele lessoniana* are evergreen and look wonderful all year. In others such as *Calamagrostis* x *acutiflora* 'Karl Foerster' the seedheads and leaves turn pale buff and remain standing like a narrow curtain, and are cut down only as the new growth emerges in spring. The leaves of miscanthus turn dry and pale in autumn, but their beautiful plumy seedheads live on into the new year.

Plant form

All grasses are monocotyledons, so they develop only fibrous root systems. Most of them are very drought-tolerant and prefer free-draining soil and a sunny position. Some such as blue fescue (*Festuca glauca*) and tufted hair grass (*Deschampsia cespitosa*) form a tight clump, which increases in size but does not spread aggressively. Others such as Bowles' golden grass (*Milium effusum* 'Aureum') spread by means of rhizomes, and some of them – for example gardener's garters (*Phalaris arundinacea* var. *picta*) – can be very invasive. It is worth checking the growth habit before deciding on a grass, because there is little worse than having a "thug" in the border. Some grasses such as *Stipa tenuissima* and *Helictotrichon sempervirens* seed quite freely, but the young seedlings can easily be pulled out when not required. Unlike other plants, grasses have their growth points at the base, so if the leaves are cut they will not regrow and are best removed.

Grasses come in many different forms: short tufted domes (such as *Carex oshimensis* 'Evergold'); arching (*Stipa calamagrostis* and pennisetums), fan-

Star performers
LEFT These grasses provide good year-round interest both from their foliage and their seedheads, which last well into winter.
1 *Stipa gigantea*
2 *Anemanthele lessoniana*
3 *Calamagrostis* x *acutiflora* 'Karl Foerster'
4 *Festuca glauca*

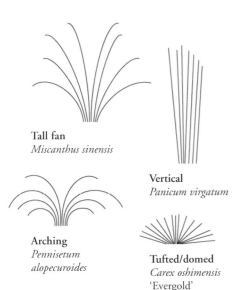

Tall fan
Miscanthus sinensis

Vertical
Panicum virgatum

Arching
*Pennisetum
alopecuroides*

Tufted/domed
Carex oshimensis
'Evergold'

Ideal companions
ABOVE Grasses in their many forms and with their soft airy textures go well with broad-leaved plants.

shaped (miscanthus); and vertical (*Calamagrostis* × *acutiflora* 'Karl Foerster' and *Panicum virgatum*).

Grasses are wind pollinated so do not need brightly coloured petals. Their flowers, however, must be able to move gently in the breeze, and this gives them a wonderfully light, fine-textured quality. Who can resist running their fingers through the silky flowers of feather grass (*Stipa tenuissima*) or *Miscanthus sinensis*?

Seasonal grasses

Grasses can be divided into warm- and cool-season growers. Warm-season ones start into growth once the soil has warmed up in late spring and flower in late summer, quickly producing seedheads that can stay on well into winter. They include molinias, miscanthus, panicums, and pennisetums. Such grasses should be divided only when growing.

Cool-season grasses start into growth early and flower in late spring and early summer; they are over by midsummer, when they become almost dormant in the warmer temperatures. This group includes festucas, helictotrichons, and most of the stipas. They can be planted or divided at almost any time of the year except the middle of summer.

New varieties
LEFT Pampas grass (*Cortaderia selloana*) – that 19th-century favourite – is now available in several smaller cultivars such as *C.s.* 'Pumila' and *C.s.* 'Albolineata', which can be used successfully as a focal point within a small garden.

GRASSES, SEDGES, AND RUSHES

Any consideration of grasses should also include sedges and rushes because these are also planted quite extensively in gardens. Knowledge of these plants will help you to find a linear-leaved plant for almost any growing conditions. While most grasses require sun and good drainage, sedges and rushes can be used in a wider variety of situations.

Grasses have cylindrical stems and are hollow except at the nodes, which are usually swollen. In some species the stem changes direction at a node.

Sedges develop solid triangular stems (remembered by the phrase "sedges have edges"). Their leaves are usually v-shaped and their flowers are less showy than those of the grasses, so they tend to be grown for their foliage effect rather than for their flowers. Some such as Bowles' golden sedge (*Carex elata* 'Aurea') are tolerant of very moist conditions, while others such as *C. buchananii* require sun and good drainage. Nearly all are evergreen.

Rushes have cylindrical stems, but these are solid and nodeless (unlike those of grasses). Many rushes such as greater woodrush (*Luzula sylvatica*) are tolerant of shade, and most require moist cool growing conditions.

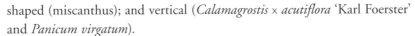

Using grasses

Grasses offer a wonderful variety of forms and textures that contrast beautifully with broad-leaved plants and flowering herbaceous perennials. Their foliage also comes in a mix of colours, ranging from silvery blue oat grass (*Helictotrichon sempervirens*), bright gold Bowles' golden sedge (*Carex elata* 'Aurea'), and bright red *Imperata cylindrica* 'Rubra' to a great array of cream and gold variegations.

Many grasses are hardy and self-sufficient plants that require little maintenance other than the cutting back or the removal of dead foliage in spring. Because they retain their seedheads, many grasses look attractive in winter when other plants have died back. They also bring a natural element into a planting scheme, because they remind gardeners so strongly of fields and open country. When selecting and planting grasses, remember that they will look at their most beautiful with the sun behind them, lighting up their flowers and seedheads.

Standing straight
ABOVE Bold clumps of buff-coloured *Calamagrostis* x *acutiflora* 'Karl Foerster' are repeated through this border and remain vertical well into winter.

Tactile treat
RIGHT Who could resist running their fingers through the wonderful billowing forms of these *Stipa tenuissima* planted in containers alongside the path?

There is a grass, sedge, or rush to suit almost every situation. Tall grasses such as *Miscanthus sinensis* or *M. sacchariflorus* can work well as a screen or informal hedge. In a mixed border tall grasses such as the cultivars of *M. sinensis*, feather reed grass (*Calamagrostis* x *acutiflora*), switch grass (*Panicum virgatum*), and purple moor grass (*Molinia caerulea*) all look good when placed at the back of the border between shrubs or tall herbaceous plants, where they can provide a contrast of form and texture. In the middle of the border use the shorter grasses such as *M.c.* subsp. *caerulea* 'Variegata', blue oat grass (*Helictotrichon sempervirens*), and pennisetums, although you do need to check the reliability and hardiness of these. At the front of the border you can use grasses as ground cover, and here they should have attractive, preferably evergreen foliage. Many species of woodrush (*Luzula*), sedge (*Carex*), and fescue (*Festuca*) make excellent ground cover plants, depending on the soil and aspect in which they grow.

Freedom reigns when it comes to selecting grasses for a naturalistic planting scheme, and as long as invasive spreaders and prolific seeders are avoided then any grasses are suitable, providing they are happy in the growing conditions. Tufted hair grass (*Deschampsia cespitosa*) is one of the few grasses that is tolerant of shade, so it can be used with many sedges and woodrushes in woodland settings alongside ferns, hostas, and hellebores.

Grasses can also make excellent plants for containers. Selection of both the container and grass will depend on the setting in which they are to be placed, but two of the most successful container-grown grasses are *Hakonechloa macra* 'Aureola' and *H.m.* 'Mediovariegata', which make soft fountain-like mounds that droop over the sides of the pot.

Plants for shade
BELOW *Carex elata* 'Aurea' (top) and *Deschampsia cespitosa* (bottom) are both tolerant of shade, so they can be used in woodland plantings to provide form, texture, and colour.

CARING FOR GRASSES

Grasses are relatively simple to look after. Although they need to be kept watered during the first year after planting, once established they should be fairly drought-tolerant. The only regular maintenance required is an annual spring grooming. Deciduous grasses should have their dead foliage cut down to ground level before the new growth emerges, and evergreen grasses should have any dead leaves or debris carefully raked out.
If you are a relative newcomer to grasses, it is a good idea to acquire one of the specialist books that has been written about grasses over the last few years, because this will really assist your planning.

An evergreen carex being tidied up during spring.

bulbs

Like herbaceous perennials and grasses, bulbs have recently experienced a great resurgence in popularity. They offer colour at almost any time of the year and so help to extend the seasons of interest in the garden into late winter and autumn, when herbaceous plants and most flowering shrubs are not performing.

The term bulb is used quite loosely here. It covers a collection of plants with swollen storage organs and includes true bulbs, corms, tubers, and rhizomes. Rhizomatous plants such as *Iris germanica* and trilliums have not been included in this section, however, because they cannot be lifted and dried off; instead they are sold in pots alongside herbaceous plants.

Many bulbs originate from regions with Mediterranean or similar climates including Turkey, the Middle East, Afghanistan, Greece, California, and South America, where long, hot dry summers are followed by cool moist winters. Under these conditions the bulbs die back after flowering, lying dormant but full of stored energy during the hot summers, waiting for the rain and cool growing conditions; then they spring into life once more. Some of these species are not fully hardy in northern Europe and are suitable for only the mildest climates or for greenhouse cultivation.

There are also other regions such as the Himalayas, China, and Japan where the winter is dry and the summer is wet, and from these have been acquired summer-flowering lilies.

The choice of bulbs available can be quite overwhelming, and it is worth sending off for a bulb catalogue so you can compare the height, colours, and flowering times of the different types of bulbs. You also need to consider how and where the bulbs are going to be planted.

Spring wonders
RIGHT During late spring alliums erupt into wonderful bobbing heads of colour in this mixed border, which includes shrubs and herbaceous plants.

Bulb cultivation
Some bulbs such as daffodils, snowdrops, and grape hyacinths are very tolerant of a wide range of growing conditions, while others such as tulips, alliums, and fritillarias require similar growing conditions to those found in their natural habitat. Drainage is the most important factor when growing bulbs, because they will not thrive in cold waterlogged soil. The addition of organic matter and sharp sand, or grit, will improve the soil structure and

Naturalistic planting
LEFT Narcissus planted in grass create charming drifts of colour in early spring. Select the small species for best effect.

drainage. Most bulbs will also do best when planted in a warm sunny sheltered situation. In gardens with heavy clay soils, some bulbs such as tulips, alliums, and lilies are best grown in containers.

Using bulbs

Bulbs can be planted in various ways within the garden, such as in a mixed planting, in a naturalistic way in grass or under trees and shrubs, or in a trough, hanging basket, or other container.

Naturalizing bulbs

Growing bulbs in grass can be a lovely method of cultivating those that can withstand competition from grass. Before buying the bulbs, however, do consider whether you are prepared to leave the grass unmown for six weeks once the bulbs have finished flowering. Try to select early-flowering bulbs such as snowdrops, species crocus, and narcissus, which finish flowering well before the grass needs cutting. Buy the species rather than cultivars; these will look far more natural and will also increase more quickly, because they can spread by seed as well as vegetatively. Plant the bulbs in drifts of the same species. Avoid buying bags of mixed bulbs as well as the large cultivars, which tend to get blown about in the wind. Bulbs for naturalizing in grass include snowdrops (*Galanthus nivalis*), species crocus (*Crocus tommasinianus* and *C. chrysanthus*), species narcissus (*Narcissus cyclamineus*, *N. bulbocodium*, *N. pseudonarcissus*, and *N. poeticus*) as well as some of the small-flowered cyclamineus cultivars such as *N.* 'February Gold'.

Naturalize bulbs that do not compete well with grass in woodland or shrub borders. Here you can grow English bluebells (*Hyacinthoides non-scripta*) – avoid the Spanish ones – wood anemones (*Anemone nemorosa*), winter aconites (*Eranthis hyemalis*), and dog-toothed violets (*Erythronium*).

PLANTING BULBS

Bulbs should be inserted deeply into the soil. A bulb 3cm (1¼in) long should be covered with 9cm (3¾in) of soil, so this means a planting hole at least 12cm (5in) deep. This prevents the bulb and in particular the flower bud from becoming frozen in a cold winter. If not planted deeply enough, bulbs will expend the energy needed for growth, pulling themselves down into the soil so may well not flower. Deeper planting also makes it harder for mice and squirrels to dig up small bulbs such as crocuses. Spacing really depends on the type of bulb and how you want the design to look when in flower. Alliums are generally well spaced out, while crocuses are planted more closely. Make sure bulbs are planted far enough apart not to touch each other.

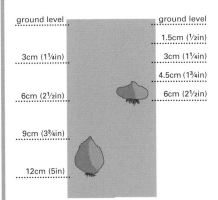

Bulbs should be planted at a depth of four times their height. Thus the large bulb (left) is deeper than the smaller one (right).

71

Mixed planting

Areas of mixed planting that include shrubs and herbaceous plants offer the ideal situation for growing some of the taller more robust and colourful bulbs. When planted between herbaceous perennials, bulbs help to disguise areas of bare soil during winter and early spring, and they can also be used to fill gaps when early-flowering herbaceous perennials such as paeonies and poppies have finished. You can have bulbs in flower from early spring through to autumn, but good drainage is essential for all of them.

Bulbs for spring colour include *Narcissus* 'Thalia', which is white and multiheaded, *Allium hollandicum* 'Purple Sensation', *Camassia leichtlinii* subsp. *leichtlinii*, crown imperial (*Fritillaria imperialis*), and tulips, which offer a wonderful array of different types of flowers, colour, heights, and flowering times. Tulips flower best when newly planted, so you should buy fresh bulbs every year. Very dark almost black ones such as *Tulipa* 'Queen of Night' have become very popular. It is best to avoid using species tulips in mixed planting, because they are usually too short; instead plant the taller later varieties such as the Darwin or lily-flowered tulips.

In summer there are several alliums that look good in mixed planting. Try *Allium cristophii* or *A. schubertii*, which produce large spherical flower heads followed by wonderful seed heads that can be cut and dried or left

Floral treat
ABOVE In summer honey-garlic (*Nectaroscordum siculum*) bears delightful bells on tall slender stems.

Sight for an artist
LEFT A mass of *Iris germanica* flower heads look like drifting blue clouds under the pergola in Monet's garden in France.

on the plants all summer. Lilies make colourful border plants, and there is a vast array of hybrids to choose from. Crocosmias offer interesting fan-shaped foliage and a range of flower colours from the traditional red of *C.* 'Lucifer' to bright yellow *C.* 'Canary Bird' and the pretty brown-marked orange flowers of *C.* 'Emily McKenzie'.

Naturalistic planting

Bulbs are used extensively in naturalistic planting schemes (see p.62), because they add seasonal change and excitement and look wonderful with herbaceous plants and grasses. All the species bulbs will prove to be tougher and more reliable than any of the cultivars, but they do need moisture in spring, followed by a good baking in light free-draining soil, once they have finished flowering. Again, with careful planning, it is possible to have bulbs in flower for many months of the year.

Tulips generally cannot be relied on to come up every year, but it is worth including a few of the small species such as *Tulipa tarda* or *T. turkestanica* in your planting scheme. Camassias with their blue spires in midspring are easy to grow, as are all the alliums. *Allium karataviense* is an interesting bulb for the front of the planting, producing two blue-grey broad leaves, followed by short spherical flowers. *Allium hollandicum* and *A. cristophii* develop their spherical flower heads in late spring, and in midsummer *A. sphaerocephalon* bears unusual egg-shaped maroon flowers on long slender stems that drift through the planting. Many other good *Allium* species are worth growing.

For height, choose honey-garlic (*Nectaroscordum siculum*). This has long stems and large clusters of bell-shaped flowers flushed pink and dark red with a greenish tinge towards the base. They will seed about very happily, and they smell deliciously of garlic.

Containers

Bulbs are ideal for planting in containers to provide spring colour. The choice of container is important. Natural materials – terracotta, stone, or wood – allow water to evaporate over the surface, so are best; avoid using plastic, because the compost stays cold and wet during winter. Containers should also be deep to prevent bulbs becoming frozen. Crock the bottom well using broken pots or polystyrene packaging, which is light and enables the pots to be moved about more easily. Select a loam-based John Innes (JI) No 2 compost and mix it two parts JI compost to one part grit (for good drainage). Do not use a peat-based potting compost, because the drainage is not good enough. To ensure a good display for several weeks, plant bulbs in layers of the same variety or use different varieties.

Cultivars of *Narcissus cyclamineus* such as *N.* 'February Gold', *N.* 'Dove Wings', and *N.* 'Jenny' are ideal for containers, as are multiheaded varieties such as *N.* 'Thalia'. Tulips are also good, and a container is the best way to grow them if you have heavy clay soil. Multiheaded tulips such as *T.* 'Georgette' and *T.* 'Angélique' and the big blousy parrot tulips are all worth a try. Be brave and experiment, and do record your successes and failures so that you can remember them for another year.

ferns

Many gardeners would consider a north-facing garden, or areas of shade within the garden, as real problems, and yet in reality they offer the opportunity to grow all those plants that thrive in shady woodland conditions. This is where ferns come into their own, offering a range of strong forms and fascinating textures that combine well with other broad-leaved shade-loving plants. Some ferns are lacy, intricate, or decorated with ruffles, while others such as hart's tongue fern (*Asplenium scolopendrium*) have more austere features. Ferns also come in many different shades of green, and some such as *Dryopteris erythrosora* produce coppery red young fronds and royal fern (*Osmunda regalis*) has rich autumn colour.

Ferns are generally very easy to grow, and most will do well in soil that is moist but well drained. They will even tolerate clay, and some adiantums will flourish in quite dry conditions. Most ferns are calcicoles (they prefer lime) or are indifferent to soil pH; however, a few such as blechnums grow better in acid soil. Most prefer shade, particularly during the hottest part of the day, and they all need shelter from cold winds. Under trees such as beech or yew the canopy may be very dense, making the soil too dry for most ferns to establish, so when planning to use such a site it is important to check it carefully before buying the plants.

When researching ferns for a planting scheme, note their forms, textures, and heights. Some such as shuttlecock fern (*Matteuccia struthiopteris*) have a strong erect fan form, while others such as polystichum are more dense and arching. The fronds may be straplike (as in *Asplenium scolopendrium*) or wonderfully divided (*Polystichum setiferum* Divisilobum Group).

Smaller ferns are most effective when planted in groups, so that they look like established colonies as they would in the wild, while the larger ones such as male fern (*Dryopteris filix-mas*), which reaches 1–1.2m (3–4ft), are best used singly where space is limited.

Another important consideration is whether the fern is deciduous or evergreen. It is really worthwhile getting to know some of the evergreen species and their cultivars, because these are invaluable in providing winter interest in shady areas in small gardens. Polystichums, polypodiums, and aspleniums are among the best of the hardy evergreen ferns, and they all have a range of interesting cultivars that will provide a contrast of different forms and textures. There are also evergreen species in some of the other fern genera, so check these out in a reliable fern book.

In a shady border, ferns will associate well with shade-loving herbaceous plants such as hostas, asarum, epimediums, astrantias, and dicentras, to provide interest at or near ground level, while shrubs such as sarcococcas, mahonias, and box can be used to create structure and winter interest. In a more open position, but where the soil remains moist and there is still some dappled shade, ferns make ideal companions for some of the taller herbaceous plants such as *Actaea simplex*, hemerocallis, *Anemone* x *hybrida*, and thalictrums.

The tree fern *Dicksonia antarctica* from the forests of Australia has become very popular over the last few years. It is like any other fern with large fronds, except that in time it produces a trunk. It can be used in the same situations as other ferns, but creates much greater impact because it can reach up to 6m (20ft). *Dicksonia antarctica* is very easy to grow and should be tolerant of temperatures down to -5°C (23°F).

Tree ferns can be particularly effective in small shady gardens or courtyards, and they make good subjects for large containers, too. They must be placed out of the wind, which can damage their fronds, and they should be watered regularly from the top so that they are kept fairly humid.

bamboos

These useful oversize grasses are well worth finding the time to study, although they must come with a cautionary warning: some are real thugs and should be avoided at all costs. Bamboos are part of the grass family, but they produce woody stems that include deposits of silica, making the stems very tough. The main structural parts of a bamboo plant are the underground system of rhizomes, the aerial culms (stems), and culm branches. The culms are unlike those found in any other woody plants, because the thickness of the emerging culm remains the same for the rest of its life and its maximum height is achieved in its first growing season.

The growth habit of a bamboo depends on these underground rhizomes. Clump-forming species ("clumpers") have short thick rhizomes, which produce a fairly tight stand of culms above ground. Running species ("runners") develop long thin rhizomes extending over great distances.

These are the more invasive species, which in some cases should be avoided. A third group – the intermediates – have root systems showing characteristics of both the other groups.

When buying a bamboo, check that there are plenty of rhizomes and healthy roots. This will indicate that the bamboo has been container grown rather then containerized (dug up and put in a pot). Young plants will establish better than large ones and will also be less expensive. Bamboos are tolerant of a wide range of soil conditions providing they are neither too dry nor too wet. Addition of organic matter before planting will ensure better establishment and growth. There is a bamboo suitable for most situations.

Bamboos are evergreen, and their height and vertical form make them ideal companions for other broad-leaved shrubs and herbaceous plants. They can be used to provide height, structure, and winter presence at the back of a border or to create a screen or division within a garden. They make an ideal screen around a children's play area, because they are tough enough for children to run through and they will swish and sigh in the wind. In a modern setting they can assume an architectural role if the culms and branches are thinned, so reinforcing the design and detailing of the garden and the hard landscaping materials. Bamboos can also be grown in containers, but their rhizomes quickly fill any pot, lowering the water-holding capacity of the soil and exhausting the supply of nutrients.

Phyllostachys are probably the most used of all the bamboos. Although they are classified as runners, in a cool temperate climate they are relatively well behaved. Their popularity is due to the wonderful coloured stems found in *P. nigra* (black), *P. aurea*, and *P. aureosulcata*.

For hedging up to 1.5m (5ft) high, think about planting fargesias, which have a tight growth habit and will need to be closely planted if a dense screen is required. Taller hedges can be successfully created from phyllostachys, pseudosasa, and semiarundinaria.

Popular options

LEFT AND FAR LEFT Bamboos can be used to provide a wide range of structural planting.

1 Most phyllostachys are good for defining areas within the garden
2 Bamboos for height and structure alongside water
3 *Phyllostachys nigra* when uplit at nighttime
4 *Phyllostachys aureosulcata* for an attractive backdrop to a seating area in a modern garden

THINNING OUT

Bamboos tend to produce dense thickets, so cutting out the old culms and branches at ground level in late spring can create a more architectural effect in a modern setting.

Phyllostachys aureosulcata f. *aureocaulis*

roses

The rose is one of the most popular and celebrated of flowers, but many people find it very hard to know which type of rose to choose from the numerous different categories. It is therefore worth having a selection of rose catalogues, particularly those listing all the shrub and species roses, and contacting the grower before you make your final choice, because they will be able to give you further help and advice.

Roses can be separated by their habit and their use in the garden into four main categories: bedding roses; shrub and species roses; climbing and rambling roses; and ground cover roses.

Bedding roses

These are the modern, large-flowered roses seen in parks and large gardens. They are very popular, and new cultivars are introduced annually. Their short stiff habit, however, makes them difficult to use with shrubs and herbaceous plants, and they are best grown on their own in formal rose beds. In order to extend the interest and cover up the bare soil, roses can be underplanted with low-growing herbaceous plants such as geraniums or be edged with lavender.

Shrub and species roses

Choose shrub and species roses for mixed borders or rose gardens. They have a softer habit, often with arching branches, and they produce flowers from soft creams and pinks to maroon and dark reds. These colours associate well with the soft-coloured plants of summer such as campanulas, geraniums, delphiniums, lavender, and lady's mantle (*Alchemilla mollis*).

Useful rose type

RIGHT Shrub roses that flower repeatedly combine well with herbaceous plants in a colourful, delicious perfumed display during the height of summer.

Most of the shrub and species roses are deliciously perfumed, and some such as *Rosa moyesii* and the rugosas produce colourful hips, extending the season of interest into autumn and providing food for the birds. When selecting roses from these groups do consider the fact that some of the older roses bear only one flush of flowers, while the modern shrub roses are repeat-flowering. This can be particularly important in a small garden. The modern shrub roses have been bred by crossing the old shrub or species roses with modern bedding ones, so making them repeat-flowering. The new roses have retained the flower shape and scent of the older roses.

Most of the shrub and species roses require little pruning. Rugosa roses make very effective informal hedges, and their foliage is very resistant to pests and diseases.

Colourful display
ABOVE Climbing roses look glorious when trained up pergola posts and then horizontally across the beams.

Informal situation
TOP A rambling rose is an ideal plant to scramble up into a tree.

Autumn hips
ABOVE The decorative hips of *Rosa rugosa* provide a source of food for birds.

Climbers and ramblers

Climbers are ideal for growing on house walls, trellis, pergolas, and tripods, while ramblers are closely related to the wild roses, and are very vigorous, so they should be used only where space allows, up trees, or on very large walls. Their flowers are very prolific but are smaller and less perfumed than climbers. They generally have only one flush of flowers, and they can also be hard to manage because they produce very long stems. Plants need pruning in late summer, after flowering. Climbers have large scented flowers and usually repeat-flower. They should be trained into a framework of horizontal branches, so slowing down the sap and ensuring maximum flowering.

Ground cover roses

These are low-growing roses that send out shoots near or along the ground. Although decorative, they are not effective ground cover because they are deciduous and offer no cover in winter. Being prickly they tend to trap leaves and debris and are difficult to work around.

ROSE CULTIVATION

All roses need a sunny open site away from trees and buildings, and shrub roses do best on well-drained soil. They all need a fair amount of maintenance, because they require feeding in order to flower well and regular deadheading and pruning. Roses can vary greatly in their susceptibility to pests and diseases – aphids, mildew, rust, and blackspot – and you should check how resistant a particular rose is before buying. A certain amount of control can be achieved through good maintenance; a regular mulch of well-rotted farmyard manure and a feed high in potassium will help to control any infections.

Blackspot causes discolouration of the leaves followed by leaf loss.

seasonal bedding plants

For added colour in the gardens at different times of the year, a gardener relies on bedding plants. A vast array of plants can be used, and the choice is very much a personal one: you may revel in a riot of bright colours, or prefer a palette of softer pinks and blues. Most bedding plants are annuals, biennials, and half-hardy perennials. An annual is a plant that flowers, sets seed, and dies all within one growing season. Its only means of survival is from seed, so it continues flowering. If you keep removing the dead flowers, then it will flower all summer, for ever trying to set seed.

Hardy annuals

Hardy annual borders used to be quite a feature in gardens. All those rather old-fashioned cottage-garden flowers are hardy annuals: for example, godetia (*Clarkia*), candytuft (*Iberis*), and love-in-a-mist (*Nigella*). These days only a few seem to be widely grown. *Cerinthe major* 'Purpurascens' with its glaucous foliage and dark maroon flowers is popular, as are cosmos, clary, and sweet peas (*Lathyrus odoratus*). Annual borders are still grown in a few large gardens, and they can be useful in providing inexpensive temporary colour before more permanent planting can be established. Hardy annuals can withstand frost so can be sown outside in early spring.

Half-hardy annuals

Many of these plants were introduced by the Victorian plant hunters and represent the "summer bedding" seen in parks and gardens – French marigolds (*Tagetes*), sages (*Salvia*), lobelia, and busy lizzies (*Impatiens*). Half-hardy annuals are not tolerant of frost, so they have to be raised under glass and planted out (traditionally at the end of spring) when all danger of frost has past. Despite being short-lived, they are very popular. Their advantage is that a colour scheme can be changed from one year to the next. If extra summer colour is needed, plant these annuals in containers.

Biennials

Plants that complete their life cycle in two years, flowering and setting seed in the second year, are known as biennials. Most of the plants used for spring colour such as wallflowers (*Erysimum*), forget-me-nots (*Myosotis*), pansies (*Viola* x *wittrockiana*), and daisy (*Bellis perennis*) cultivars are treated as biennials and discarded after flowering. They make ideal companions for spring-flowering bulbs in the garden or in pots.

Half-hardy perennials

These are the larger more woody plants such as pelargoniums, fuchsias, argyranthemums, cannas, dahlias, and coleus, and like annuals they are invaluable in containers. They would survive outside all year in a warmer climate, but more generally they have to be brought in and overwintered in a heated conservatory or greenhouse. With milder winters in temperate areas, many of these half-hardy plants are now surviving out of doors in sheltered gardens. Using these plants does create extra work for the gardener, and restricting their use to containers is usually the most successful way of introducing extra colour into the garden.

Reliable self-seeder

ABOVE LEFT Love-in-a-mist (*Nigella damascena*), here with roses, will seed itself happily from year to year.

Useful biennials

ABOVE CENTRE Forget-me-nots make a colourful blue carpet below these white spring-flowering tulips.

Annuals for the potager

ABOVE RIGHT Sweet peas (*Lathyrus odoratus*) and pot marigolds (*Calendula*) create a "potager" effect when grown among vegetables.

Seasonal splendour

LEFT Cannas and dahlias form an exuberant design in late summer, with other half-hardy bedding plants.

There are some important factors to consider when choosing plants for a particular garden or landscape. The plants must not only suit the site conditions so that they establish successfully and really thrive, but they must also fulfil a particular role within the site – be it screening out a poor view, providing enclosure around a small garden, or integrating large buildings or a domestic dwelling into the local environment. Plants are dynamic so these changes will be difficult to manage if suitable plants have not been selected for the site and if maintenance is not considered during the planning stages.

3 plant selection

naming and identifying plants

In order for any artist to be truly creative they must understand the materials they are working with. The same is true for gardeners if they are to create successful planting schemes. Also, a visit to any foreign country is enhanced by the possession of a little knowledge and the ability to speak a few words of the language. Think how much more enjoyable a visit to the garden centre or nursery will be if you know some botanical Latin and can readily identify a range of plants. Latin names may seem rather frightening at first, but once you have mastered a few words you will soon discover that identifying and naming plants is actually fun.

The binomial system

Botanical Latin is an international language and allows botanists and plants people worldwide to communicate, regardless of their native language. It is used on plant labels in botanical gardens, such as Kew, and in the RHS gardens at Wisley, both in Surrey, UK, as well as in garden centres.

A binomial system of naming plants was introduced by Carl Linnaeus in 1753. Under this system every individual plant is given two Latin names – a genus and a species – hence the term binomial (two names). Linnaeus, however, began his classification by grouping plants into families according to the structure of their flowers and fruit, and irrespective of whether each plant was a tree, shrub, or herbaceous perennial. The family Rosaceae, for example, includes plants as seemingly diverse as roses, apples, hawthorn, cotoneaster, and strawberries, but they all have a similar flower structure with five petals. The family name always starts with a capital letter and ends in "-aceae".

Genus Each family is divided into smaller groups each called a genus (plural genera). There may be as many as 1,000 genera in a family (for example, Asteraceae – the daisy family) or as few as one genus (for example, Eucryphiaceae). A genus name always starts with a capital letter and is equivalent to your own surname. It is the first name of the binomial system, and it appears in italics, or is underlined if hand written: for example, *Quercus* is the genus for oak trees.

Species Every plant in a genus is then given its own second name, a species name, which is equivalent to your forename. A species is a plant that occurs naturally in the wild and will always reproduce itself exactly from seed: for example, common oak (*Quercus robur*), common ash (*Fraxinus excelsior*), and common beech (*Fagus sylvatica*) are all species of temperate trees that will come true from seed.

The species name always starts with a small letter, and it appears in italics, or is underlined if hand written. It may describe some characteristic about the plant such as the colour of its flowers (for example, *purpurea* for a purple-flowered plant), its country of origin (*japonica* for a plant native to Japan), or the person who collected it in the wild or introduced it into gardens (for example, *wilsonii* for a plant that was collected by the Victorian plant hunter Ernest Wilson).

FAMILY ROSACEAE

This comprises a wide range of plants but they all have a similar flower structure with five petals. Some such as apples, plums, and strawberries provide wonderful edible fruit, while decorative rowan berries are food only for birds. Roses are renowned for their beautiful flowers and scent, and the flowers of perennial lady's mantle are loved by flower arrangers.

Apples
(*Malus*)

Plums, cherries
(*Prunus*)

Rose names

Each of the thousands of roses in the genus *Rosa* has its own name, many of which identify its origin.

Rosa banksiae was named after Lady Dorothea Banks, wife of plant collector and director of Kew Gardens in the UK, Sir Joseph Banks.

In *Rosa canina*, *canina* means "dog". Native dog rose is so called because it has no smell and is therefore considered inferior.

In *Rosa glauca* (left), *glauca* means "blue/green", which is the colour of the leaves.

In *Rosa rugosa*, *rugosa* means "wrinkled/rough", which is the texture of the foliage.

SPECIES NAMES

There are many other examples where the species name is helpful in identifying the plant. It could relate to the shape or size of the leaf, the size of the plant, the scent given off by the flowers or foliage, or the fact that a plant displays similar characteristics to another plant.

Ajuga reptans
reptans "creeping" (spreads by creeping along the ground)

Betula pendula
pendula "hanging down"

Buxus sempervirens
sempervirens "evergreen"

Choisya ternata
ternata "in threes" (leaves in clusters of three)

Cyclamen hederifolium
hederifolium "ivy-like leaves"

Galanthus nivalis
nivalis "snow white"

Lavandula dentata
dentata "toothed" (as in toothed leaves)

Macleaya cordata (right)
cordata "heart-shaped"

Osmanthus heterophyllus
heterophyllus "different-shaped leaves"

Populus alba
alba "white"

Thymus citriodorus
citriodorus "lemon scented"

Viola cornuta
cornuta "horned flowers"

Hawthorns
(*Crataegus*)

Roses
(*Rosa*)

Rowans, whitebeams
(*Sorbus*)

Strawberries
(*Fragaria*)

Lady's mantle
(*Alchemilla*)

Cultivars

While many plants have only two names, numerous others have more than that to differentiate them from the original species. They may have occurred spontaneously in the garden by genetic mutation or they will have been specially created by plant breeders. Many of these plants are known as cultivated varieties, or cultivars. Unlike a species, a cultivar does not reproduce itself exactly from seed, so it must always be propagated vegetatively from cuttings, grafting, or some other method whereby material is collected from the parent plant.

A cultivar name always appears in Roman type within single quotation marks and starts with a capital letter: for example, *Rosa rugosa* 'Alba' and *Hosta* 'Sum and Substance'. Cultivar names used to be Latinized, but they are now written in the language of the country of origin.

A cultivar may not always be the best or most suitable plant to grow in your garden, because often a species will grow faster and tolerate a wider range of growing conditions than a cultivar. The plant expert Beth Chatto in her garden in Essex, UK, for example, grows a very wide range of species that thrive in her particular conditions.

Hybrid plants

Some species when grown together in the wild or in cultivation are found to interbreed and form hybrids. These are called inter-specific hybrids and are recognized by an "×" placed between the genus name and the species name. Examples of inter-specific hybrids that are readily available to gardeners are *Photinia* × *fraseri* 'Red Robin' and *Viburnum* × *burkwoodii*. Very occasionally a cross occurs between two genera, and this is called an

Country of origin name
The German name *Sedum* 'Herbstfreude' is now used instead of *S.* 'Autumn Joy'.

Compatible bedfellows
LEFT Species requiring very well-drained conditions and an open sunny site grow happily together in the dry gravel garden.

inter-generic hybrid. The most famous of these is the dreaded leylandii cypress X *Cupressocyparis leylandii* – an inter-generic hybrid being written with a large "X" at the start of the name. This extremely fast-growing conifer has been so overplanted and misused that in some countries legislation has had to be introduced to restrict its height and use.

Pronunciation of botanical Latin

Many people become quite anxious about the correct way to say a Latin plant name, even though many such names are already in everyday use: antirrhinum, nasturtium, rhododendron, and dianthus, for example, cause no problems, so be brave and just have a go. There is often no right or wrong pronunciation, but it may help to practise saying the name aloud to hear how it sounds.

Plant identification

Knowing how to recognize a plant is an invaluable skill, whether the plant is in your own garden or elsewhere. A good gardener always has a notebook to hand, and these days a digital camera is also a wonderful tool to help record the details of a plant you want to remember. If it is permissible to take a flower or leaf then do so – there is nothing like having a piece of plant in front of you when you get home.

If you are to become a knowledgeable gardener, you need to equip yourself with at least one specialist book on trees, shrubs, herbaceous plants, and bulbs as well as a large plant encyclopedia. Some of these books have keys to flower and leaf types, while others show plants in chronological order so that you can find those of interest at a particular time of year.

Name changes

Changes in long-established names are a nuisance for every gardener, especially when the new name is much harder to learn and remember. There are generally good reasons for the name changes, though, so you just have to accept them and try to learn them.

Know your plants
ABOVE *Photinia* x *fraseri* 'Red Robin' (top) can easily be identified by its bright red new foliage, which later turns green, while *Berberis* x *ottawensis* f. *purpurea* 'Superba' (bottom) is an inter-specific hybrid, that is a cross between two species so has characteristics of both.

WHAT TO LOOK FOR

Inevitably it is easiest to identify a plant when it is in leaf or flower. At other times of year the stems and fruits or seeds will help you pinpoint a plant, while learning to look at the arrangement of the branches, the buds, and the characteristics of twigs and bark are particularly important for trees in winter. This is also where the characteristics of plant families will come in useful.

The structure of the tulip-like flowers of *Liriodendron tulipifera* actually place it in Magnoliaceae (the magnolia family).

Seed capsules of *Iris foetidissima*.

site analysis

Before designing your garden, you need to consider the following factors: those relating to the site and which therefore impose themselves on plant selection; and those concerning the plants themselves – their uses as well as their horticultural and visual merits, which may make them suitable for a particular place. Location can greatly affect plant choice, especially if it is important to work with the "genius loci" (the spirit of the place). You should therefore note whether the site is in a rural or urban area.

A rural setting could be that of rolling hills, of the vast open skies above low-lying countryside, or of breaking waves on the coast. In such places, check out the vistas, because the most important factor could be retaining a wonderful view out of the garden and ensuring that the boundaries of the garden are as discreet as possible. This would mean selecting appropriate natives or cultivars of natives around the boundaries so that the garden and landscape merge, creating a "borrowed landscape". Thus, in a rural setting you should avoid trees with coloured foliage or very coarse texture around the boundaries, because they demand attention and separate the garden from the landscape.

In an exposed coastal site the salt-laden wind may be a real problem, so a priority here would be to establish a windbreak in order to create some shelter for both plants and people. In this situation you should check out those plants that are tolerant of salt sea spray. Take your lead from the plants growing locally, and in coastal areas you will see sea buckthorn (*Hippophae rhamnoides*) and *Euonymus japonicus* frequently used as hedging.

In the city, town, or suburb, your garden and other outdoor spaces should relate more closely to the built environment and the architecture. Rows of semi-detached houses or city skyscrapers need softening and greening up, and here it is possible to use a much wider range of ornamental plants. These garden or urban spaces are contrived, more like stage sets where

borrowed landscape

city view

almost anything goes. Cars will also dominate these areas, and often the role of the garden designer is to combine space for cars with places for people.

Here also the architecture will usually influence the overall design of the site, so it is important to work with this. In a city centre the massive scale of the buildings will influence the type of plants selected, because the plants will need to be in scale with the buildings, whereas in a suburban environment the architecture will be on a smaller, more domestic scale, and the planting will reflect this.

In all locations there may be a view such as an ugly building or roof line that requires screening out. Here it is important to select a tree such as *Fraxinus angustifolia* 'Raywood' or a hedge of hornbeam (*Carpinus betulus*), which will merge into the scene and not draw attention to the view behind.

A modern problem is that of road noise, and this can affect a rural or urban garden. If space allows, a dense planting of evergreen trees and shrubs can help alleviate this nuisance, but this is much harder to do in a small space. Often the best that can be achieved is a hedge of something evergreen such as *Viburnum tinus*, where the dense foliage helps to absorb the noise.

Borrowed landscape
FAR LEFT Because no boundary is visible, the garden can merge seamlessly into the fields beyond.

City view
LEFT In this urban roof garden, the design, materials, and plants reflect the architecture of the buildings around.

Softening effect
BELOW In a suburban front garden a hedge creates enclosure while ornamental planting blurs and softens the parking space for cars.

RECORDING INFORMATION

Walk around both the inside and outside of the site noting all the information that you will need when making your plant selection. Have a checklist as an *aide-mémoire*. Create a photographic record of all the features and existing planting, so that you can refer back to this when drawing up your design for the garden.

softening effect

use of the site

The type of site, whether it is your garden, an amenity area such as a public park or square, or a commercial site surrounding shops or factories, will affect your selection of plants.

In your garden the most important factor when deciding on plants will be how you propose to use and maintain the site. The requirements of individual family members should be considered, and if there are children and dogs the planting needs to be robust and not easily trampled underfoot. You may want to create shade, scent, or screening around a sitting area and have a separate play area for the children and another one for growing fruit or vegetables. Other members of your family may well want to be involved in the plant selection, and their likes and dislikes will influence the choice of plants. In a family garden it is best to avoid plants that are poisonous or have sap that can cause skin irritations like the euphorbias.

A public space will present a very different set of criteria. It often has an extensive areas of grass for recreational purposes, and trees will be needed to create height, provide shade, and define routeways. The planting of public spaces should be varied, with some good robust areas of planting but also some more ornamental beds and borders to provide seasonal interest and excitement for its users. The planting once established must be tough and tolerant of a wide range of weather conditions as well as a certain amount of vandalism and pollution. It should also be relatively low maintenance. The budget will be a major factor in public planting, so plant selection will be quite cost-driven. This usually means choosing readily available low-cost plants and using them in closely planted blocks.

Public parks and squares are an exciting challenge for today's designers and park managers. Within these spaces there should be some ornamental planting, and Victorian bedding schemes do still live on in some parks and squares, providing seasonal colour. Many managers, however, are now using the more naturalistic style of herbaceous planting first seen in the German parks. Others are planting hardy annuals and wild flower meadows. These schemes are easier to maintain than bedding and also cost far less.

Form, texture, and evergreen structure should play a very important role in most public space planting, while colour and flowers will be of much less importance. In Parc André-Citroën in Paris, France, there are some wonderful examples of public planting, such as where birch trees have been underplanted with densely planted box clipped into cubes of random height, and on the other side drifts of lavender and perovskia create a welcome sea of pale purple.

private gardens

Private gardens
LEFT Ornamental planting encloses the eating area in this family garden, softening its edges and also creating seasonal interest for diners.

commercial sites

Commercial sites
LEFT Strong forms, textures, and seasonal colour define walkways and soften buildings, creating a pleasant human environment.

Public parks
BELOW In Parc André-Citroën, in Paris, *Betula utilis* var. *jacquemontii* has been combined with clipped box, for a modern and stunning effect.

public parks

The planting and "greening" of commercial sites such as shopping centres and business parks are now an important part of the whole development process. Plants are used to soften the large-scale buildings, making them less intrusive, and to provide a pleasanter environment for people to work in. The planting should conceal the buildings both from outside the site and within; it should also enclose and screen car parks, define roads and walkways, and provide height and visual interest in large areas of hard landscaping. The scale of the site and the planting are very important, because often the buildings are of considerable height so large trees have to be used. Pleached trees are often introduced, to give privacy to the people working in the buildings. The soil may well be poor on these sites, so robust trees and shrubs are necessary. On some sites the soil may previously have been contaminated, and it is therefore worth checking out the depth of new soil before ordering plants for the site. Also ensure that you have plans that show all the underground services, because these could interfere with tree plantings. Good examples of successful commercial sites are at Stockley Park near Heathrow, UK, and at La Défense in Paris, France.

historic site · Mediterranean style

style, mood, and theme

The style of a site will be influenced not only by its location but also by the associated architecture, and an important part of any site analysis is making a photographic record of all the buildings on the site. The architecture affects the style, scale, colour, and materials in the planting.

The style of the garden can be formal, informal, or asymmetrical, and this will often be decided by the look of the building, and the planting should reinforce this. Strong shapes such as domes, spires, or rectangles that occur in the building or the design of the garden could be reflected by using clipped or strong natural forms in the planting scheme. On a historic site the decision to restore the garden or landscape back to its original style will drive the plant selection, as can be seen in the Privy Garden at Hampton Court, in the UK, and at Het Loo in Holland.

If the design has a strong mood or theme such as cottage, Mediterranean, gravel, water, or minimalist, then this should be followed through into the style of planting. A cottage garden would have a very traditional selection of plants: a climbing rose around the door, fruit trees, herbaceous plants, and some vegetables in the borders. To reinforce the sleek lines and crisp materials in a minimalist garden you would need a simple design with strong

minimalist theme **house–garden link**

Historic site

OPPOSITE LEFT The formally laid-out design of this chateau garden at Villandry, in France, reinforces the style and historic nature of the buildings.

Mediterranean style

OPPOSITE RIGHT The domes used in the planting repeat the shapes of the architecture and ground plan, as well as the distant hills near Nice, in France.

forms and textures, perhaps using blocks of plants such as grasses or clipped box cubes, a few coloured bamboos with the lower stems removed, pleached lime trees, or the beautiful trunks of paper-bark maple (*Acer griseum*).

On very bland sites, for example in some suburban family gardens, where there is no particularly strong style or theme, then you really need to decide on the mood or flavour that you want to create. Try to visualize the end result and how you want the planting to look, because it is impossible to be creative when you are working in a vacuum. In a front garden you can consider what you would like to offer guests when they arrive at the house or people passing by. In a back garden you may be able to link the planting back to something you have seen in the house, for example a picture or the colour of the curtains.

Minimalist theme

ABOVE LEFT The bold forms and soft textures of the planting scheme complement and reinforce the crisp lines in this garden.

House–garden link

ABOVE RIGHT Here the eye is led out to the garden, creating a strong connection between indoor and outdoor spaces.

93

understanding soil

As well as aspect, soil is another major factor that determines the plants that thrive on any given site. Attitudes to planting have changed over the last 25 years; whereas once people would dig in vast quantities of peat or apply iron sequestrene to their borders in the hope of growing acid-lovers such as azaleas or rhododendrons, it has now been realized that the most successful approach to gardening is to go along with the natural growing conditions and select only those plants that thrive in them. This in turn means that you should spend time looking up plant origins and checking to see the growing conditions required by each plant. The more scientific approach ensures that far more plants establish successfully, but first it is necessary to understand how the soil, its structure, and preparation relate to satisfactory plant growth.

Studying the topsoil

The first thing to check in your garden is the depth of topsoil. This is the fertile "living" part of the soil, the layer where organic matter is present, as well as the soil bacteria that break down the organic matter into humus and release its nutrients back into the soil. Topsoil can vary in depth from a few centimetres to a metre. To assess the depth of the topsoil, dig a small pit 60cm (24in) deep and look at the exposed soil. The topsoil will show up as a darker layer in which plant roots are visible. Below this is the subsoil, which is lacking in humus and plant nutrients. It is worth digging several pits in different parts of the site. For shrubs and herbaceous plants 30cm (12in) of topsoil is required. Grass will grow on as little as 7.5cm (3in), and trees tolerate shallow soil as long as a generous planting pit has been prepared and the subsoil broken up.

If the topsoil is very thin it may be necessary to buy in additional topsoil, but this should be of a similar type to that already in your garden. If a soil pan is present this will show up as a severely compacted layer about 30cm (12in) below the surface. It is often responsible for poor drainage, and it is necessary to break up the hardpan by double digging or deep rotavating and the addition of organic matter.

Soil texture

The texture is the relative amounts of sand, silt, and clay particles present in the soil. It is these particles that give the soil its characteristics and its name. Because it is virtually impossible to change soil texture, its type will determine which plants will grow most happily on a given site. The texture can be assessed by rubbing the soil between your fingers. Moist sandy soil will feel gritty, silt is silky, while clay soil when wet can be pressed into a sausage shape.

Assessing the drainage

Plants that grow well in the hot dry conditions of the Mediterranean require good drainage. Having their roots in cold, wet heavy soil during winter usually spells death to all the silver and grey plants, as well as to bulbs such as tulips that also require well-drained soil. It is poor drainage rather than temperature that kills off plants such as penstemons.

On very heavy soils it may be necessary to install a piped drainage system to lower the water table and encourage deeper rooting and provide a better soil environment for plants.

Checking soil pH

The soil pH is a measure of the acidity or alkalinity in the soil. The scale is from 0 to 14, but most soils lie within the range 4.5–8.5. For good plant growth the optimum pH is 6.5, because at this point most of the plant nutrients are readily available. You should check out the pH of the soil at several different areas of your garden, because it may vary. If you do find your garden has soil with a low or high pH then you have the marvellous

acid-lovers

lime-lovers

The structure of the soil is the way the soil particles hold together. A sandy soil has a light open structure that drains well and warms up quickly, while a clay soil usually has a poor structure that holds a lot of water, making it cold and heavy. Because the texture of a soil cannot readily be changed, it is the structure that has to be improved. The easiest way to improve soil structure is to dig in well-rotted manure. Grit can also be used and is ideal when planting bulbs or small plants that require free-draining soil. However, it is expensive on a large scale.

opportunity to grow those plants that will thrive in those specific conditions.

Acid-lovers and lime-lovers

Most plants in the family Ericaceae are unable to grow on soil containing lime, because it inhibits the uptake of iron in these plants and their new leaves become yellow and chlorotic. These acid-loving plants require a pH range of 4.0–5.5. During your initial assessment of the garden try to look around at the other plants that are growing in the area, because this will be a good guide as to the type of soil in the locality. If pieris or heathers are growing well then this may indicate an acid soil.

Some plants prefer a high pH, of over 7, that is, chalky alkaline soils. This group of lime-lovers includes clematis, scabious, and daphnes. Many of the plants that grow on limey soils in fact need the free drainage that goes with these soils, rather than having an actual requirement for a high pH.

Nutrients in the soil

It is important that sufficient nutrients are available for plant growth, and these can be added as organic or inorganic fertilizers. Phosphorus encourages good root development, nitrogen develops healthy green leaf growth, and potassium encourages flower and fruit development. Unless you know that a soil has been contaminated, or suspect some nutrient deficiency, it is not usual to check the nutrient status of a soil.

Acid-lovers and lime-lovers

ABOVE Most rhododendrons (left) require acid soil (pH 4–5.5), while buddlejas (right) thrive on the good drainage found on alkaline soils over pH 7.0.

Plants for acid soil

Acer palmatum

Camellia japonica

Erica x *darleyensis*

Pachysandra terminalis

Pieris sp.

Rhododendron sp. and cvs

Plants for alkaline soil

Buddleja sp.

Chimonanthus praecox

Clematis sp. and cvs

Daphne odora

Scabiosa caucasica

Adding organic matter while digging will help improve soil structure.

ecological planting

A ttitudes to gardening and growing plants have changed considerably over the last 50 years. Gardening as well as visiting gardens and shows such as the Chelsea Flower Show and Hampton Court, in the UK, have all become part of the way of life, as has watching TV gardening programmes and visiting garden centres. People who have no garden strive to grow flowers and vegetables in containers on balconies and small patios.

Many of the plants grown have also changed. At one time cultivars were the popular choice of gardeners, and plant breeders strove to produce plants with ever larger, more colourful flowers. These plants were often of unknown parentage, and it was difficult to find any helpful information about the growing conditions required. The Chelsea Flower Show seemed full of azalea and rhododendron displays, which was very misleading, because gardeners assumed they could grow these plants in their own garden. Unfortunately,

ecological garden

too, many plants on sale in garden centres had very limited cultural advice on the label. Gardeners were beguiled into buying plants on display because they had wonderful flowers or coloured foliage, and even if there was advice on the label they often paid little heed to it. Once purchased these plants often struggled to survive, because they were being grown in the wrong soil or aspect.

Nowadays though, thanks to plant experts such as Beth Chatto and Piet Oudolf, the emphasis is very much on growing the "right plant in the right place". This has brought about the introduction of more species plants that have been found growing in the wild. The nurserymen who

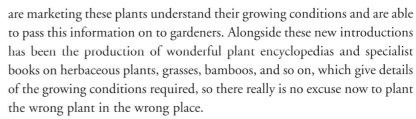

are marketing these plants understand their growing conditions and are able to pass this information on to gardeners. Alongside these new introductions has been the production of wonderful plant encyclopedias and specialist books on herbaceous plants, grasses, bamboos, and so on, which give details of the growing conditions required, so there really is no excuse now to plant the wrong plant in the wrong place.

Once you have analysed your soil and decided whether it is a heavy clay or a light free-draining soil, and noted which are the sunny areas and which shady, you can then select your plants. Start this process by checking where each possible plant comes from. Their origins can be found in a good plant encyclopedia. If a plant comes from sunny, dry rocky areas in Turkey then alarm bells should ring if you had hoped to grow it in a shady, north-facing garden on damp heavy clay. In the wild you would never see a soft green fern that requires moisture and shade growing alongside a lavender that needs sun and good drainage, so you must not expect them to be able to do this in your own garden.

You should always be striving to grow together those plants that originate from similar habitats. It doesn't matter if they are from different countries. Providing they all require similar growing conditions, then they will grow happily side by side and will with time look like a natural plant community. How satisfying this will be both for plants and gardener. There is simply no point in trying to change the soil or the growing conditions in your garden.

Fantasy garden
FAR LEFT A garden with roses round the doorway, and all manner of other plants and ornamentation, will have to remain a dream. It is simply not appropriate in most gardens.

Ecological garden
LEFT Natural materials and simple planting create an ecological water garden that will fit happily in the landscape and also attract wildlife.

99

plant adaptation

It is worth taking the time to discover the adaptations shown by plants growing in different habitats, because this can really help with plant selection. Unlike humans, plants are unable to move out of the hot midday sun or find water when they are drying out. Only the fittest survive, and those plants that have managed to adapt to a particular set of growing conditions are the ones that are still around today. Plants have had to make further adaptations where their habitats such as peat bogs and forests have been destroyed or where there has been excessive applications of nitrogen-rich fertilizers on arable land.

Shade plants

Plants that tolerate shade are usually from woodland areas where light levels will be low once the tree canopy is out in spring. The soil will be rich in organic matter and moist, although there could be dry areas around the base of trees.

Plants growing in shade have often adapted to these conditions by developing large, dark green leaves, giving a large surface area and increased chlorophyll. These factors enable them to make the best use of any light and to photosynthesize efficiently. Leaves may have a shiny waxy cuticle to reflect light onto other leaves and to reduce water loss. They may be cut or finely divided, allowing light to pass through to other leaves, or the plant may creep along the ground so that its leaves receive more light. Some plants may climb upwards towards the light. Most plants flower early in the year before the tree canopy is out.

Mediterranean-climate plants

The growing conditions typical of Mediterranean areas are of intense sunlight for most of the summer coupled with little or no rain. In such conditions many plants have silver or grey leaves to reflect the light, helping them to stay cool, while others have small or rolled leaves to reduce the surface area and cut down water loss. Some leaves develop hairy surfaces to trap moisture and slow down transpiration, and others produce aromatic oils for similar reasons. Bulbs and other storage organs allow some plants to survive stressful periods underground.

Alpine plants

True alpines are those plants growing above the tree line. Snow in winter is followed by a period of wet as the snow melts in late spring. The water is moving, however, and alpine plants cannot survive in permanently wet soil. The light is very bright and often there are strong winds.

Plants tolerating these conditions are usually ground hugging with small leaves to cut down water loss. Some may have silver or shiny leaves to reflect light and sunken stomata to trap moisture. Those found in scree beds are larger but will still show similar adaptations.

Desert plants

In deserts, there is likely to be intense sunlight, virtually no rain, and a low level of nutrients. To cope with these conditions, many plants such as cacti have actually lost their leaves, and their stems, which are green, have taken on the role of photosynthesis. The plants have strange shapes so that, as the sun moves round, one part of the plant shades another. The leaves and stems are fleshy and able to store water, and are often prickly in self-defence. Following rain they can flower and produce seed in a matter of hours.

Plant adaptations

RIGHT Shade plants have large, dark green leaves, and in Mediterranean plants the leaves are small, silver, and sometimes hairy. Alpine plants are small-leaved ground huggers, while desert plants are leafless and develop strangely shaped, spiky stems.

shade

Mediterranean

alpine

desert

the role of planting

Once you have carefully researched the origins and climatic suitability of plants for your garden, you then need to refine the list further by thinking about the role of the plants that you are wanting to use.

Visual qualities

The first consideration will be the structural planting – the trees, shrubs, and hedges that will provide the third dimension, the height, within the garden (see pp.40–3). The amount of structural planting will vary greatly on different sites but will include plants for screening, creating privacy and seclusion, providing shelter, division of space, creating a backdrop, reinforcing or screening boundaries, creating a woodland or habitat for wildlife, or providing shade. Where there is existing planting on site, particularly trees, try to ensure that any new plants fit well with this, and that all the plants reinforce the overall design and the mood or style of the garden.

You can then move on to the ornamental, focal-point, and ground cover planting (see pp.44–81). When selecting trees, remember that the canopy will cast shade, and this will affect the light levels and the plants underneath. A silver birch (*Betula pendula*), for example, has a light airy canopy while the Norway maple *Acer platanoides* 'Crimson King' has a dense canopy beneath which very little will grow.

As you select the other plants decide on whether you require them to be evergreen or deciduous, and check that you have enough winter structure. It is important particularly in a small garden to consider what each plant looks like in winter – does it disappear and leave bare soil. Think about the form of the plant (see pp.12–13) or the flowers if herbaceous (see pp.14–15). Then consider its texture, colour, and shape (see pp.16–37). For ornamental plants you should study all the seasonal aspects: flowers, fruit, coloured foliage, autumn colour, and coloured stems.

Horticultural qualities

At the same time as you are researching the visual qualities of a plant you also need to check out its horticultural qualities. This will ensure that you

structural planting

ornamental planting

really are matching the plant to the site. In order to do this, it is really worth investing in a good plant encyclopedia – it will prove to be money well spent. The cultivation information there will describe each plant's requirements, enabling you to decide if a plant suits your soil, drainage, aspect, and wind exposure. If you are used to gardening in a particularly mild part of the country and then move to a colder area, do pay particular attention to the details about frost hardiness.

When choosing a tree it is particularly important to note its eventual height and spread. A tree will not always conform to the exact dimensions given in a book, but it will enable you to decide whether it is a large, medium, or small tree. All too often an inappropriate tree is planted in a small space, and in later years has to be felled, or undergo such drastic pruning that its natural form is completely destroyed.

Trees and shrubs such as ornamental crab apples or some acers that produce fruit, berries, or large leaves can become a nuisance in autumn, especially after heavy rain. The fruit and leaves can collect on a busy path or road, making it slippery and dangerous, and some fruit such as of mulberry (*Morus nigra*) can cause unsightly stains on paving materials. Trees for a patio also need to be selected with care if the area is to be used for eating. Those such as flowering cherries that drop petals or have messy seeds that break up on the tree, such as birch, can make the area look untidy and create extra maintenance. In a small garden avoid plants with a suckering or invasive growth habit such as macleaya, which may run under fences and turn up in the neighbour's garden.

Plant choice is particularly important in gardens where there are young children and in public places, where you must avoid plants that have poisonous fruits or seeds such as laburnum or aconitum, and euphorbias that exude a sticky, latex-like substance that can cause severe skin irritation. Another plant that can cause problems is Jerusalem sage (*Phlomis fruticosa*), because, like *Fremontodendron* 'California Glory', it has a hairy covering on its stems and if inhaled can cause breathing difficulties.

Finally, when making your plant selection, do check out the plant's availability in the current edition of the *RHS Plant Finder*. Where your budget is limited go for plants that can easily be sourced, because they will be less expensive. The best advice, though, to ensure a successful planting scheme is to get to know your plants, the growing conditions they require, and their visual and horticultural qualities so they can play the role for which you chose them.

winter colour

Structural planting
OPPOSITE LEFT Plants that create a green backdrop are needed in any garden.

Ornamental planting
OPPOSITE RIGHT Plants for seasonal excitement and colour enhance a garden.

Winter colour
FAR LEFT Winter can still be an attractive time if the right plants are selected.

Extra maintenance
LEFT Messy trees can increase the amount of work required.

factors affecting plant growth

In order to ensure the successful establishment and growth of plants it is essential to take time and trouble improving the planting site, adopting the appropriate planting techniques, and doing regular maintenance.

Soil preparation and planting

It is vital to clear the planting site of all perennial weeds, because it is very hard to eradicate them once planting has been done. Weeds will compete with the plants for water, nutrients, and light and may also harbour pests and disease.

There is always the temptation to overplant a new border. When the plants first go in there seems to be a large area of bare soil. Plants need space to grow and planting too closely will create competition and spoil the natural form of the plant. All plants will grow towards the light, so if planting is too dense the plants will become drawn and leggy and they will struggle to flower.

Once the ground has been thoroughly dug, the soil structure improved by the addition of organic matter such as well-rotted farmyard manure, and fertilizers added as appropriate, the planting can be done. You must always remove any dead, damaged, or diseased stems and roots, and hammer in the tree stake before planting the tree in the hole, and securing it to the stake.

Plants must be watered well after planting, and a 10cm (4in) layer of mulch such as shredded bark will help to cut down water loss and prevent weed growth. It is important to apply sufficient water around a plant so that it reaches the roots. A light sprinkling of water just encourages the roots to come to the surface, making them more susceptible to drought.

Plant aftercare

Wind can do serious damage to plants as can frost, so newly planted evergreens could be protected with horticultural fleece, or on a large site a proprietary windbreak material could be erected temporarily and then removed once the plants are established. It is also important to check that newly planted trees and shrubs are well firmed in so that on a windy day they do not suffer root rock. Trees will need at least 9 litres (2 gallons) of water several times a week during dry weather. Regular weeding particularly during the first year is very important – weeds can quickly spread through a bed or border swamping the cultivated plants. It is also important to check for pests and diseases and take the appropriate action as soon as possible, because both can be detrimental to plant growth.

The application of fertilizer will depend on the soil and the type of plants being grown, but flowering plants and bulbs will benefit from a dose of potassium to promote flowering and flower colour.

Formative pruning with the removal of any inward-growing or crossing branches may be necessary as a tree or shrub grows, to ensure it develops a well-balanced form. Any dead, damaged, or diseased wood should also be regularly removed, and tree ties checked and loosened as the tree grows.

Other factors affecting plant growth

Mowing or strimming too close to the base of a tree will injure the bark and inhibit the growth on the damaged side of the tree. A tree guard will prevent this damage and in rural situations will also prevent wounds caused by deer and rabbits nibbling at young tree bark.

In towns and cities plants may be susceptible to vandalism. Desire lines where people or animals take the short cut across a new area of planting should be avoided by good planning of paths at the design stage of the project. If new planting is likely to be damaged then a temporary fence should be erected until plants are established. Planting large trees that create an immediate impact can also prevent the harm that is sometimes done to smaller trees when branches are snapped off.

The need for maintenance

LEFT Good or bad maintenance can affect establishment and plant growth.

1 A badly prepared border in which Japanese knotweed (*Fallopia japonica*) is emerging among new planting

2 Mulching a border with organic matter will reduce maintenance and improve moisture retention

3 Poor planning can lead to the creation of desire lines when plants get trampled under foot

4 A newly planted area in which plants have been well spaced out, giving them enough room to develop

5 Tender plants should be wrapped in horticultural fleece to protect them from cold winds and frost damage

6 Watch out for diseases and pests such as slugs or snails, which have eaten these hosta leaves

7 This bark wound has been caused by mowing or strimming too close to the trunk of a tree

8 A tree guard prevents damage to a young tree from deer and rabbits

9 Prune out any inward-growing or crossing branches as the tree grows so that it develops a well-formed crown

105

Creating a planting plan is a really important part of any garden-design project because it helps you to develop your ideas on paper and to visualize the effect you would like to achieve in the garden. It also enables you to think your plant selection through very carefully, thereby ensuring that you have a successful planting scheme that provides all-year interest in the garden. A planting plan is useful, too, when organizing the planting itself, such as when deciding on how much space each plant requires and how many plants should be purchased.

4 planting plans

preliminary stages

A planting plan is a scaled drawing of a bed or border, showing all the plants you have selected and where you intend to plant them. Creating your first planting plan is rather like learning to drive. You need to learn the rules to help you get started, and then as you grow more confident you can break free and experiment with different ideas.

On a planting plan most plants are represented as simple circles (see pp.112–13) with their names written in the circles or alongside. Such a plan must be neatly presented with the plant names clearly legible, because it will be used to set the plants out in the garden.

Site assessment

If possible, do the site assessment on a sunny day during the growing season, when you can see areas of sun and shade and identify the existing plants more readily. The first stage is to measure up the area(s) to be planted with a metric tape. Also note the aspect for the site, using a compass. Aspect is very important because it will dominate your plant selection (see pp.94–5). Make a checklist to ensure you record everything about the site that could affect your planting (see pp.88–97). Failure to do an accurate assessment may lead to plant loss.

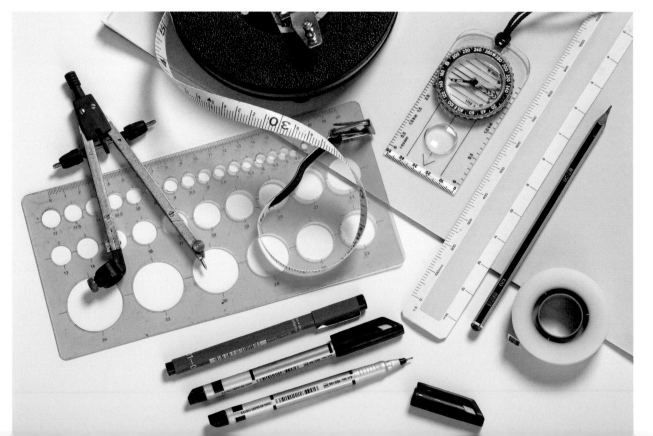

EQUIPMENT
You need the following equipment before you begin a planting plan. All items are readily available from high street stores.
- metric tape to measure the garden
- orientation compass to note north and south
- scale rule with 1:50 and 1:100, although you could use a metric ruler
- tracing paper
- circle guide
- compass with pen attachment
- three good-quality fibre pens in these thicknesses: fine (0.25mm), medium (0.3mm), and thick (0.5mm)
- hard (2H) pencil for detailed work, and a soft (B) pencil or a charcoal one for sketching
- roll of sticky insulating tape
- drawing board (optional)

SKETCHING PLANT FORMS

Before you start to think about specific plants, practise drawing a range of plant forms and textures (see pp.12–21). Using a soft (B) pencil or a charcoal one, draw four simple forms that are often seen in plants: a round/oval, conical form, hummock, and dome. Then change the outline of the shapes to suggest different textures. A "fine oval" could represent *Osmanthus delavayi* while a "coarse oval" could be *Fatsia japonica*. Once plants have been selected for a particular site, you can then work three dimensionally, drawing in the forms and textures of the plants and seeing how they will work together.

Round/oval

Fine-textured oval

Medium-textured oval

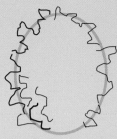

Coarse-textured oval

Conical form

Fine-textured conical form

Medium-textured conical form

Coarse-textured conical form

PLANTING SITE TO SCALE

Draw up the area to be planted using the scale rule. With a scale of 1:50; 1m on the ground is represented by 2cm on the plan (1yd by 0.72in). Mark where north is so that you are clear about the aspect of the site.

Hummock

Fine-textured hummock

Medium-textured hummock

Coarse-textured hummock

Dome

Fine-textured dome

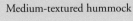

Medium-textured dome

Coarse-textured dome

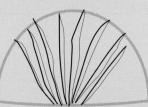
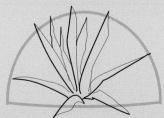

109

planting in triangles

When you design any planting scheme you need to think about how you would like the site to look and whether there is to be a strong theme or style to the garden, such as naturalistic or modern (see pp.128–65). Then decide where you want the tallest plants to go and how the evergreen structural planting will be arranged (see pp.40–3). The easiest way to do this is to sketch some elevation drawings at scale 1:50 showing the planting in triangles so that you have groups of plants that work together, with tall ones at the back and low plants grounding the taller ones.

Making an elevation drawing

Always try to plan the planting in layers so that you have a mixture of tall, medium, and low-growing plants. In order to do this you need to ensure that beds and borders are wide enough to accommodate more than one plant's width so there is sufficient space for shrubs, herbaceous plants, and ground cover planting. Once you have drawn the triangle showing where the proposed mature height will be, you can then fill the elevation drawing with the various forms and textures that are to be combined. Do not think about individual plants at this stage – just concentrate on composing the broader picture, placing the plants at the front so they partially hide those farther back in the bed or border. Remember to include some accent, or focal-point, plants that will draw the eye into the planting.

Plant selection

Once the elevation drawing is satisfactory, you can select the plants for that site. A wide range of books and plant catalogues is needed at this stage in planning. Try to restrict yourself to plants that are widely available, and avoid choosing plants you know nothing about. Compile lists of plants that you would like to use that suit the site theme and conditions. You may find

Symmetrical planting triangle
RIGHT The planting is evenly balanced and therefore fairly static because the eye focuses on the whole group of plants. In a long border that is viewed from the front you could use a series of symmetrical triangles so that the height is evenly distributed along the length of the border with lower plants linking each of the groups.

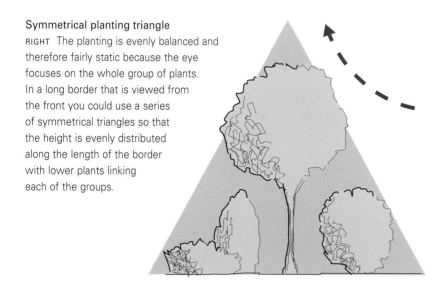

Asymmetrical planting triangle
RIGHT Here, the tallest planting is towards one side of the border, creating movement upwards to the peak of the triangle and then down again towards the ground. This asymmetrical style of planting can be very successful in a short border or small bed.

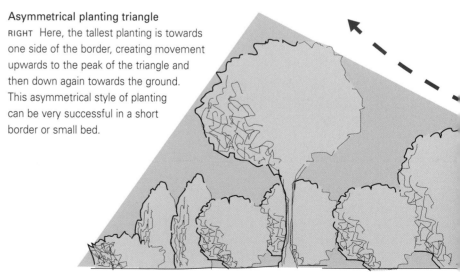

it helpful to create a table of plants and their characteristics. These headings might prove useful:

- large structural evergreen shrubs (more than 1m/3ft) for back of border
- medium evergreen shrubs (up to 1m/3ft) for midborder structure
- low-growing evergreen shrubs for ground cover/front of border
- tall herbaceous, grasses, and ferns for back of border (1m/3ft plus)
- ornamental shrubs (seasonal interest from foliage, flowers, fruit)
- herbaceous plants, grasses, ferns for midborder (under 1m/3ft)
- low-growing herbaceous plants, grasses, ferns for ground cover and front of border
- bulbs

Create separate tables for different beds and borders in the garden. Although the final number of plants will be decided by the size of each site, you will probably include far more plants than you eventually use. Then refer back to your elevation drawing and choose plants from the table that fit the required form, texture, and height.

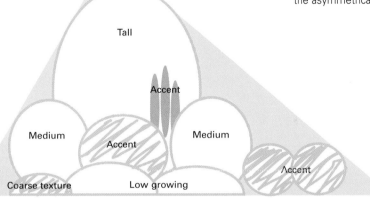

Preliminary elevation drawing
BELOW Within the triangle draw in the rough shapes of the plants. You need to think about the forms, textures, and the visual balance of the planting. In this group there is strong accent planting in the centre, while the other accent plants on the lower right of the group draw the eye outwards and downwards completing the asymmetrical triangle.

Creating a table
RIGHT Use the headings suggested above to compile a table of plant characteristics, in which you note the main features of each plant, based on information gleaned from encyclopedias and plant catalogues.

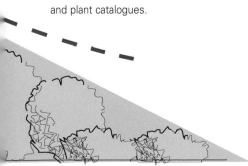

PLANT CHARACTERISTICS							
	Evergreen/ Deciduous	Height/ Spread	Circle guide	Interesting attributes	Form	Texture	Colour
LARGE SHRUBS FOR STRUCTURE AT BACK OF BORDER							
Elaeagnus x *ebbingei*	Evergreen	2m/1.5m+ (6½ft/5ft)	20	Grows quickly; heavily scented flowers	Upright	Medium	Creamy flowers in autumn; silvery leaves
MEDIUM SHRUBS FOR MIDBORDER STRUCTURE							
Viburnum davidii	Evergreen	1m/1m (3ft/3ft)	12	Low branches cover ground well	Dome	Coarse ribbed	Dark green leaves

111

use of circles

On a planting plan, each plant is represented by a circle, in the centre of which is a cross (+) to indicate the exact planting spot. The diameter of the circle is selected according to the planting distance, and this is determined by the eventual size and spread of the plant. Reference books and catalogues will give quite variable measurements particularly for the ultimate height and spread of shrubs, and the growing conditions will also affect them. It is therefore easiest to use a limited number of planting-distance circle sizes. If you keep to these, the scheme will start to look fairly mature in about four years providing the soil has been well prepared.

Use the circle guide to draw appropriately sized circles on the planting plan. Circles should touch but must not overlap. When grouping several plants together, the circles are linked together (see opposite). Each plant circle should be labelled with the relevant plant name, written horizontally. If at all possible, include the name within the circle(s). If you do have to draw a line from the circle to a plant label, make sure the line is neat and as short as possible. When using more than one plant write in the number of plants in that circle: for example, three *Alchemilla mollis* or five *Tellima grandiflora*.

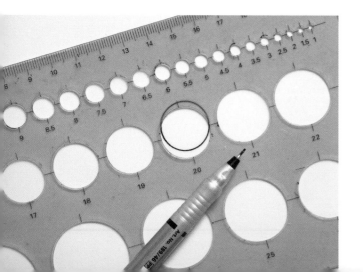

Circle guide
LEFT A simple way to show planting distances on a planting plan is to draw them through a circle guide.

30cm (12in): circle size 6
Use for herbaceous plants that remain small and do not spread: e.g. *Verbena bonariensis, Festuca glauca*.

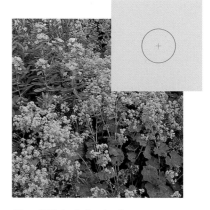

45cm (18in): circle size 9
Use for most herbaceous plants that will spread and create a bold group: e.g. *Alchemilla mollis, Heuchera* 'Greenfinch'.

60cm (24in): circle size 12
Use for large/spreading herbaceous plants or small shrubs: e.g. *Sedum* 'Herbstfreude', *Viburnum davidii*.

100cm (36in): circle size 20
Use for large shrubs: e.g. *Phormium tenax, Prunus lusitanica*, and all shrub roses.

CIRCLE SIZES FOR HERBACEOUS PLANTS AND SHRUBS

Type of plant	Planting distance	Circle guide hole size	
Small herbaceous plants, grasses, and ferns that do not spread *Aconitum* 'Stainless Steel', *Asarum europaeum*, *Bergenia* 'Silberlicht', *Epimedium* x *youngianum* 'Niveum', *Tellima grandiflora*, *Viola* sp. and cvs	30cm (12in)	6	
Most medium-sized herbaceous plants and grasses *Alchemilla mollis*, *Anemone* x *hybrida* 'Honorine Jobert', *Brunnera macrophylla*, *Luzula sylvatica*, *Polystichum aculeatum*	45cm (18in)	9	
Large herbaceous plants, ferns, and grasses that spread *Achillea filipendulina* cvs, *Dryopteris affinis*, *Geranium macrorrhizum*, *Matteuccia struthiopteris*, *Miscanthus sinensis*, *Polystichum setiferum*, *Calamagrostis* x *acutiflora*	60cm (24in)	12	
Shrubs less than 1,000mm (36in) high that grow slowly and remain small *Buxus sempervirens* 'Suffruticosa, *Euonymus fortunei* 'Emerald Gaiety', *Sarcococca* sp., *Skimmia* x *confusa* 'Kew Green', *Phormium* cvs, *Pinus mugo* 'Gnom', *Viburnum davidii*	60cm (24in)	12	
Shrubs more than 1,000mm (36in) high. Could reach almost any size if left unpruned *Fatsia japonica*, *Viburnum tinus*, *Prunus lusitanica*, *Mahonia japonica*, *Elaeagnus* x *ebbingei*, *Osmanthus* x *burkwoodii*	100cm (36in)	20	
Shrub roses more than 1,000mm (36in) high Species roses, old and modern shrub roses, *Rosa rugosa*, *R. moyesii*, *R.* 'Nevada', *R.* 'William Lobb', *R.* Gertrude Jekyll	100cm (36in)	20	
Wall shrubs and climbers with height and spread less than 2m (6½ft) *Clematis viticella*, x *Fatshedera lizei*, *Lonicera* x *brownii* 'Dropmore Scarlet'	2m (6½ft)	see p.114	
Wall shrubs and climbers with height and spread more than 3m (10ft) *Garrya elliptica*, *Clematis armandii*, *Ceanothus arboreus* 'Trewithen Blue', *Hydrangea anomala* subsp. *petiolaris*, *Parthenocissus henryana*	3m (10ft)	see p.114	

DRAWING PLANT GROUPS

With a soft (B) pencil and the circle guide, draw a series of touching circles at the appropriate planting-distance circle size. Use a fine (0.25mm) fibre pen to write in the plant name, number of plants, and a cross (+), followed by a medium (0.35mm) fibre pen to ink in the finished outline of the plant circles.

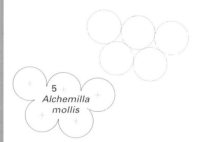

Showing a plant group.
Form individual circles for each plant and then link them together, inking in the group outline.

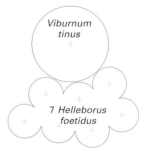

Different plant types
When placing, for example, a group of herbaceous plants next to a large shrub, the circles should still only touch.

drawing styles and colouring

Trees, climbing plants, wall shrubs, and hedges are depicted in a different way to other plants on a planting plan, because trees are likely to overshadow parts of a planting, while climbers are often encouraged to scramble through structural shrubs. At the back of the border, wall shrubs can be trained over a wall or fence, while hedges depend on the plants being used and the desired effect. All their shapes on the planting plan therefore reflect the way they are to be grown. To do this, mark the planting-position cross (+) for each climber or shrub 30cm (12in) away from the wall or fence, and around it draw the appropriate outline shape, depending on whether it is a climber or a wall shrub or hedge to be pruned or left informal (see below). Mark the planting-position cross for single-row hedges, such as of yew or thuja, about 90cm (36in) apart. For a fairly dense hedge of hornbeam or beech, insert a staggered double row of crosses.

Garrya elliptica — Informal wall shrub

Pyracantha cv — Clipped wall shrub

Hedera helix 'Glacier' — Climbing plant

Clematis montana — *Cotoneaster salicifolius* 'Rothschildianus'

Clipped hedge

Planting around a tree

BELOW It is important to plant under trees in order to avoid large areas of bare soil. Although newly planted trees cast little shade initially, you should still leave a clear space of 1m (3ft) around the trunk to reduce competition for nutrients and moisture. The planting may have to be changed as the canopy spreads and casts more shade. Under mature trees the soil may be very dry, and also dense fibrous roots may make planting tricky. Dry shade is the most difficult situation to plant.

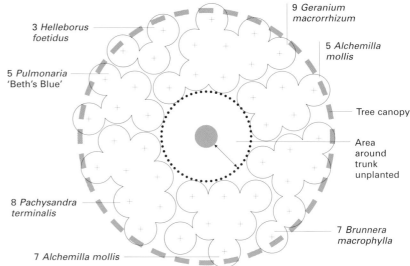

3 *Helleborus foetidus*

9 *Geranium macrorrhizum*

5 *Alchemilla mollis*

5 *Pulmonaria* 'Beth's Blue'

Tree canopy

Area around trunk unplanted

8 *Pachysandra terminalis*

7 *Brunnera macrophylla*

7 *Alchemilla mollis*

Wall shrub, climber, and hedge outline shapes

LEFT Use the appropriate outline shape on your planting plan to represent a wall shrub, climber, or hedge and the way it is to be grown. Shrubs may extend out into the border, so allow sufficient space for this on the plan. A formal clipped hedge needs a crisp outline style, while an informal hedge can be more loosely drawn.

Adding colour and interest

Planting plans are normally drawn onto tracing paper and then photocopied, although specialist computer software can also do the job efficiently. When working for someone else, keep the original trace and present the photocopy to your client. If you feel the plan looks a little dull, you can add some colour to the photocopy. This is best done with coloured pencils, because photocopy paper is often very thin and does not take water colour well. Buy good-quality coloured pencils with soft leads and apply some colour very sparingly around the edge of the circles. Ensure that the plant names can still be easily read.

Further interest can also be created on a planting plan by restyling the outline of the various plant groups so it shows, for example, the textural qualities of the foliage. This is done when you come to ink up your drawing on the tracing paper.

Extra information
BELOW LEFT Colour, suggesting flower or foliage tints, has been added around the edge of these plant groups, so the plan is easier for the client to read.

Textural interest
BELOW RIGHT Here the textural qualities of the plants has been indicated by changing the outline of the plant groups. *Alchemilla mollis* has large soft foliage so has been given a soft outline, while *Carex* and *Luzula* are represented with spiky outlines.

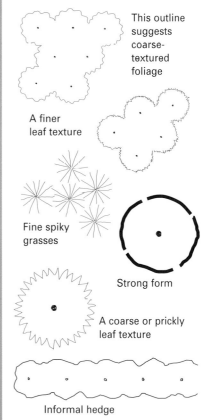

FOLIAGE STYLE OUTLINES

Using different outlines for plant groups makes a planting plan more readily understood and also helps to communicate your ideas to a client. It is a quicker technique than adding colour. The outline can show a form and/or texture, and you can always exaggerate the differences on plants with similar characteristics.

This outline suggests coarse-textured foliage

A finer leaf texture

Fine spiky grasses

Strong form

A coarse or prickly leaf texture

Informal hedge

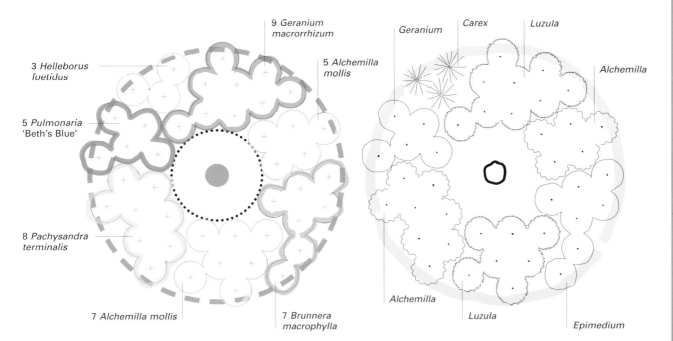

3 *Helleborus foetidus*

9 *Geranium macrorrhizum*

5 *Alchemilla mollis*

5 *Pulmonaria* 'Beth's Blue'

8 *Pachysandra terminalis*

7 *Alchemilla mollis*

7 *Brunnera macrophylla*

Geranium

Carex

Luzula

Alchemilla

Alchemilla

Luzula

Epimedium

back, front, and midborder

When actually drawing the plant shapes on the planting plan, try to work in an organized way. Think of the bed or border as a sandwich: bread (structural plants) at the back, bread (ground cover plants) at the front, and the filling (ornamental plants) in between.

Back of border

Leave an additional 1m (3ft) between large structural shrubs to allow for their size once fully mature. Then interplant them with tall herbaceous plants such as *Anemone* x *hybrida* 'Honorine Jobert', grasses such as *Miscanthus sinensis,* or ferns such as *Dryopteris affinis*. These can always be removed at a later date as the shrubs start to expand into the space. Although the tall herbaceous plants should be selected for their flower form, it is helpful if they also possess interesting foliage and form (see pp.12–13). Plant these in groups or drifts.

In a small or medium-sized garden the large shrubs, especially when evergreen, are generally planted as single specimens, because blocks of such

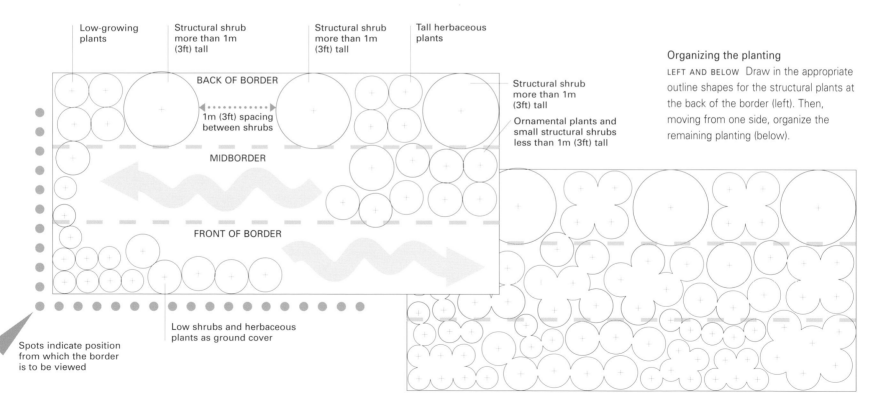

Low-growing plants

Structural shrub more than 1m (3ft) tall

Structural shrub more than 1m (3ft) tall

Tall herbaceous plants

BACK OF BORDER

1m (3ft) spacing between shrubs

MIDBORDER

FRONT OF BORDER

Structural shrub more than 1m (3ft) tall

Ornamental plants and small structural shrubs less than 1m (3ft) tall

Low shrubs and herbaceous plants as ground cover

Spots indicate position from which the border is to be viewed

Organizing the planting
LEFT AND BELOW Draw in the appropriate outline shapes for the structural plants at the back of the border (left). Then, moving from one side, organize the remaining planting (below).

shrubs can look very heavy. Wall shrubs can be used instead of freestanding shrubs, and climbing plants positioned between the structural shrubs to provide extra height and seasonal interest.

Front of border

The plants at the front of the border should be mostly low-growing ground cover, preferably evergreen with good foliage and form: for example, *Bergenia* cultivars, *Tellima grandiflora*, or *Euonymus fortunei* 'Emerald Gaiety'. Flowers are a bonus. In larger borders it may be appropriate to bring some tall airy plants, such as *Verbena bonariensis* or *Calamagrostis* x *acutiflora*, to the front in order to create visual interest and prevent the planting becoming too regimented. Plants at the front should be planted in groups or drifts; avoid using single plants. They should be placed so there is no bare soil once the plants have established.

Midborder

In the space between the tall structural planting and the ground cover, introduce some smaller evergreen shrubs, such as *Viburnum davidii*, *Sarcococca confusa*, or *Hebe* 'Mrs Winder', to provide midborder structure. Then select some ornamental plants to create seasonal excitement and colour with their flowers and foliage. Depending on the size of the border these ornamental plants will be deciduous shrubs or herbaceous plants and grasses. Use herbaceous plants and smaller grasses in groups or drifts, except for short-season plants such as paeonies or poppies, which are best planted singly and repeated along the border.

Plants that flower early in the season such as *Dicentra spectabilis*, lupins, and poppies are best positioned towards the back of the border, because once they have finished flowering they either disappear or become untidy and need to be hidden by other plants.

The following pages describe four different planting requirements – a shady border; a dry, Mediterranean bed; a naturalistic border; and a minimalist one – and how to interpret them on a planting plan.

USE OF REPETITION IN PLANT DESIGN

- When plants are used more than once in a bed or border, this gives a satisfactory sense of rhythm within the planting. It could be the same plant that is repeated or a different cultivar of that plant such as *Bergenia* 'Silberlicht' and then *Bergenia* 'Beethoven'. When designing a border that is sunny in parts and shady in others try to repeat textures, for example a grass such as *Anemanthele lessoniana* in the sun and a grass-like plant such as a woodrush (*Luzula sylvatica*) in the shade.
- when a border is to be viewed from the sides as well as the front, remember to place low-growing and medium-sized plants at both border sides to ground the taller plants.
- by repeating structural plants within a border, interest will be maintained once the main growing season is over and deciduous and herbaceous plants have died down. If there are large areas of bare soil in winter then rethink your planting.
- sometimes the backdrop will dictate how the planting is arranged. If for example there is an attractive brick wall at the back of the border that needs to be on view, then less structural planting is required at the back.

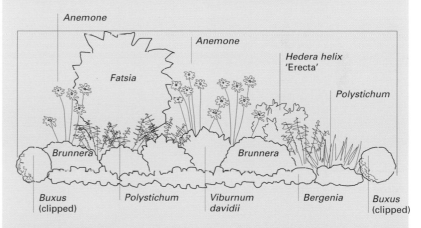

Balanced composition
A sense of rhythm and repetition has been achieved by planting more than one anemone, polystichum, brunnera, and clipped box along the border.

shady bed planting plan

The brief is to suggest a planting scheme for a bed that is close to the back of a terraced townhouse. The bed lies in the north-east corner and receives virtually no sun, and there is an area of paving, 2m (6½ft) wide, between the bed and the house. The planting needs to look good all year and have winter interest from foliage and scented flowers. It will be seen from the house and from within the garden.

The bed is 5m (15ft) wide and 2.5m (8⅓ft) deep, and is backed by an unattractive panel fence, 2m (6½ft) in height, which needs to be hidden behind the planting. The soil is moist and pH 6.5 (very slightly acid).

Tackling the brief for a shady bed

- decide on how you would like the planting to look.
- because this is a shady bed, the choice of plants will be limited to those that can tolerate low light levels, that is, woodland plants. The emphasis will be on foliage forms and textures, and any flowers will appear mostly between late winter and early spring. The planting needs to have interest that can be appreciated from the house in winter.
- start to plan the bed thinking in triangles and where the height will be. Because the fence is unattractive and needs to be hidden behind the planting, a series of interlocking triangles will probably work best. This means that the structural evergreen shrubs should be spaced out along the length of the border.

Doing an elevation drawing

- once you have gathered your initial thoughts, sketch them in an elevation drawiang, showing how the forms and textures will combine to give an interesting planting scheme. The planting needs to have a focal point; in this instance it will be a coarse-textured plant such as *Fatsia japonica* or *Mahonia* x *media* 'Charity'.

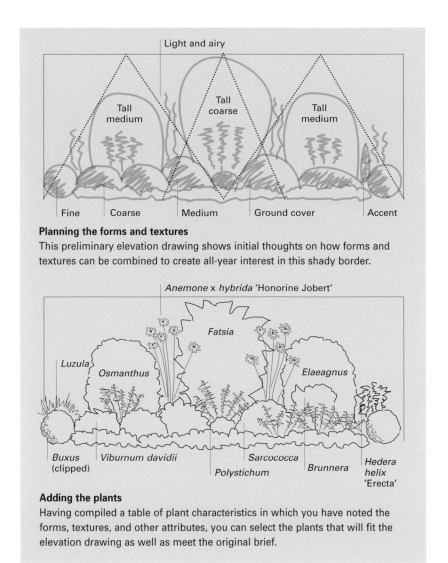

Planning the forms and textures
This preliminary elevation drawing shows initial thoughts on how forms and textures can be combined to create all-year interest in this shady border.

Adding the plants
Having compiled a table of plant characteristics in which you have noted the forms, textures, and other attributes, you can select the plants that will fit the elevation drawing as well as meet the original brief.

- then work out on the elevation drawing how forms and textures can be combined to create all-year interest.
- once the elevation drawing has been done, you can start to research specific plants that would be suitable for this shady bed.
- decide on the headings for the table of plant characterstics (see p.111) and select your plants beginning with the evergreen structural plants for the back of the border. Once you have chosen enough plants under each of the headings, close the books and catalogues. Working from these lists, put specific botanical names to the plants shown on the elevation drawing, thinking about the height, form, and texture of each plant.

Creating the planting plan

- when you are happy with the plant selection, try to represent your plants in plan form, that is, how they will be set out on the ground. Place a piece of tracing paper over the outline of the border that you drew to scale (see p.109).
- beginning at the back of the border, that is, with the structural evergreen shrubs, make a rough sketch of the planting plan. Pencil in a circular area for each larger plant, then mark in the other plants with appropriately shaped and labelled drifts or clouds.
- once you are satisfied with the arrangement of the plants in your shady border, you can use the circle guide to draw in the individual plants on the actual planting plan using the H (hard) pencil (see pp.112–13).
- it is always a good idea to shade in the evergreen plants to check that there is enough foliage structure and winter presence within the design.

Drawing a rough planting plan
ABOVE RIGHT Larger shrubs appear as approximate circles while the smaller plants are shown as drifts in the rough sketch of the planting scheme.

Completing the planting plan
BELOW RIGHT Once satisfied with the plant selection use the circle guide to draw in all the plants. Link the smaller circles together to create drifts. Shade the evergreens.

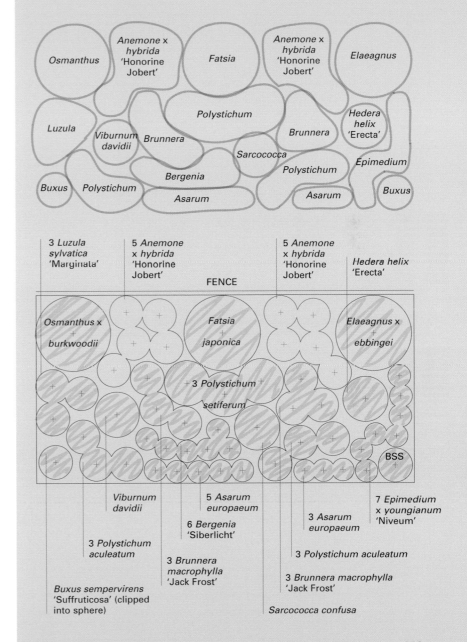

dry, Mediterranean planting plan

This dry, Mediterranean bed is to be in a sunny open position on free-draining soil of pH 6.5, with an annual rainfall of less than 63cm (25in). The bed, 7m (23ft) wide and 5m (16ft) deep, can be walked around and viewed from all sides. Once planted it will be mulched with gravel to retain moisture and keep maintenance to a minimum. The growing conditions are therefore ideal for those plants originating from the Mediterranean – the silver-

and grey-leaved plants and tough plants with small leaves that are adapted to surviving strong sunlight and low rainfall (see pp.136–9).

The stages in drawing up a planting plan are exactly the same as for the shady bed (see pp.118–19). Once a triangle has been drawn to scale so it shows where the height will be, possible forms and textures are sketched in before plant research is done and specific plants chosen.

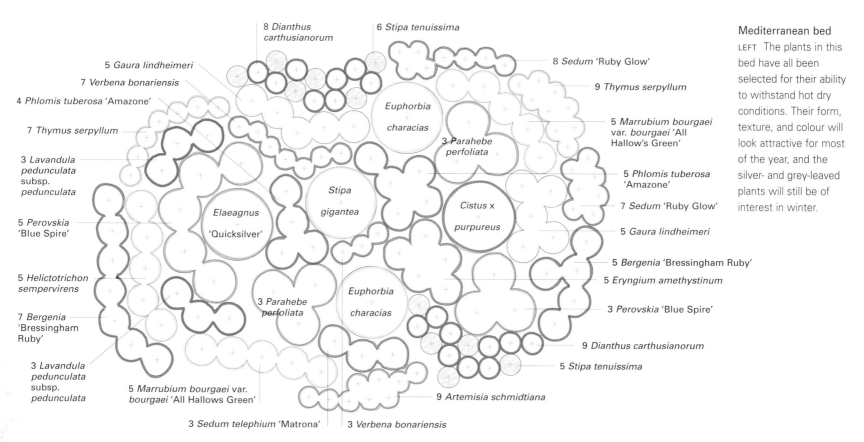

8 *Dianthus carthusianorum*

6 *Stipa tenuissima*

5 *Gaura lindheimeri*

7 *Verbena bonariensis*

4 *Phlomis tuberosa* 'Amazone'

7 *Thymus serpyllum*

3 *Lavandula pedunculata* subsp. *pedunculata*

5 *Perovskia* 'Blue Spire'

5 *Helictotrichon sempervirens*

7 *Bergenia* 'Bressingham Ruby'

3 *Lavandula pedunculata* subsp. *pedunculata*

5 *Marrubium bourgaei* var. *bourgaei* 'All Hallows Green'

3 *Sedum telephium* 'Matrona'

3 *Verbena bonariensis*

Euphorbia characias

3 *Parahebe perfoliata*

Stipa gigantea

Elaeagnus 'Quicksilver'

Cistus x purpureus

3 *Parahebe perfoliata*

Euphorbia characias

9 *Artemisia schmidtiana*

8 *Sedum* 'Ruby Glow'

9 *Thymus serpyllum*

5 *Marrubium bourgaei* var. *bourgaei* 'All Hallow's Green'

5 *Phlomis tuberosa* 'Amazone'

7 *Sedum* 'Ruby Glow'

5 *Gaura lindheimeri*

5 *Bergenia* 'Bressingham Ruby'

5 *Eryngium amethystinum*

3 *Perovskia* 'Blue Spire'

9 *Dianthus carthusianorum*

5 *Stipa tenuissima*

Mediterranean bed

LEFT The plants in this bed have all been selected for their ability to withstand hot dry conditions. Their form, texture, and colour will look attractive for most of the year, and the silver- and grey-leaved plants will still be of interest in winter.

In this dry, Mediterranean bed the height is provided by *Elaeagnus* 'Quicksilver', a deciduous shrub that closely resembles an olive tree. The other structure is provided by *Cistus* × *purpureus* and *Euphorbia characias*. All the plants will provide interesting forms, textures, and colour from foliage, flowers, and seedheads well into winter. Low-growing plants such as bergenias, thymes, and sedums soften the edge of the bed. Bulbs can be planted for extra seasonal colour.

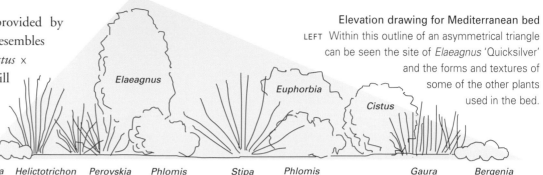

Elevation drawing for Mediterranean bed
LEFT Within this outline of an asymmetrical triangle can be seen the site of *Elaeagnus* 'Quicksilver' and the forms and textures of some of the other plants used in the bed.

Bergenia Helictotrichon Perovskia Phlomis Stipa Phlomis Gaura Bergenia

BULBS

Bulbous plants can only be planted between the shrubs and herbaceous plants, and they will go in last. In the Mediteranean bed, they can be put between the gaura, verbena, phlomis, and dianthus. Bulbs, too, need to be marked on the planting plan, but their rough positions can first be sketched on an overlay.

- if you are planting only a limited range of bulbs in small numbers, just write the name of the bulb alongside the planting plan. Never attempt to show individual bulbs on a planting plan.

- if a large number of bulbs are to be used, take a piece of tracing paper and, securing it over the planting plan, create an overlay that shows exactly where the drifts of bulbs are to be planted. Indicate the number of bulbs within each drift.

- in order to calculate the number of bulbs in each drift, decide on the effect you want to achieve with the bulbs – are they to be loosely or densely spaced – and then research the planting distance of the bulbs. Calculate the number of each bulb required for each square metre (square yard). Work out the area of each drift, and then calculate the number of bulbs you will need to plant there.

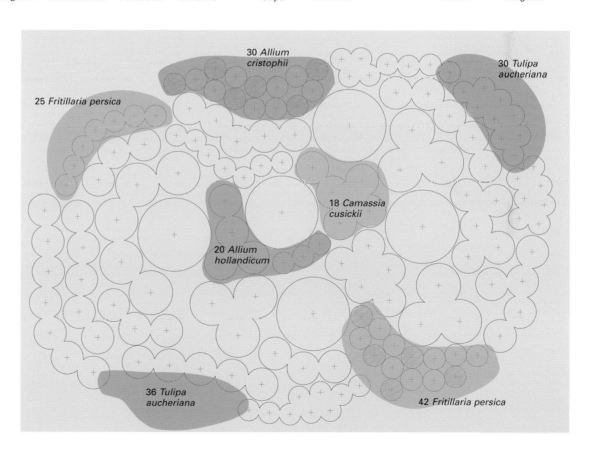

30 *Allium cristophii*

25 *Fritillaria persica*

30 *Tulipa aucheriana*

18 *Camassia cusickii*

20 *Allium hollandicum*

36 *Tulipa aucheriana*

42 *Fritillaria persica*

naturalistic planting plan

This bed of 8.5m (28ft) wide and 6.5m (22ft) deep is part of a larger planting scheme and is in the spirit of the new-wave, naturalistic planting style (see pp.134–5). The designer's brief is for an open sunny bed on light, free-draining soil of pH 6.5. The basic stages in meeting this brief and creating a planting plan are as for the shady bed (see pp.118–19).

Although the planting in this instance has been planned on a grid, once the plants grow and spread they will begin to fuse and the geometry will be lost. Overall bed structure is provided by the hornbeam hedge at the back and along one side of the bed. To fit the requested theme, all the plants are herbaceous perennials or grasses, and many will produce attractive seedheads that will remain during winter, only being cut back in late winter before the new growth begins. To create a rather more relaxed looking planting plan, the textural qualities of the plants can be suggested by varying the plant outlines: a drift of grasses such as miscanthus could have a slightly spiky shape, while *Sedum telephium* 'Munstead Red' would have a softer one.

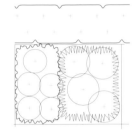

Drawing in the drifts
RIGHT Pencil in individual plant circles, and mark each planting-position cross (+) with a fine (0.25mm) fibre pen. By then inking around the whole drift, a softer outline is achieved on the planting plan.

Ornamental grasses
LEFT *Stipa gigantea* creates a light airy feel at the back of this new-wave border, while veronicastrum, phlox, salvia, and thalictrum reveal their stronger flower forms and colour.

Planting plan for naturalistic bed

RIGHT A low hornbeam hedge provides the backdrop and structure for this perennial bed. Its chosen plants will display their interesting forms and seedheads during the winter months. The evergreen grass *Sesleria nitida* has been planted to create a neat edging in front of the nepeta and trifolium, both of which will need cutting back in autumn.

Sedum telephium 'Munstead Red'

Helianthus salicifolius

Change of colour

LEFT As autumn approaches the golden colour of seedheads begins to dominate this naturalistic border.

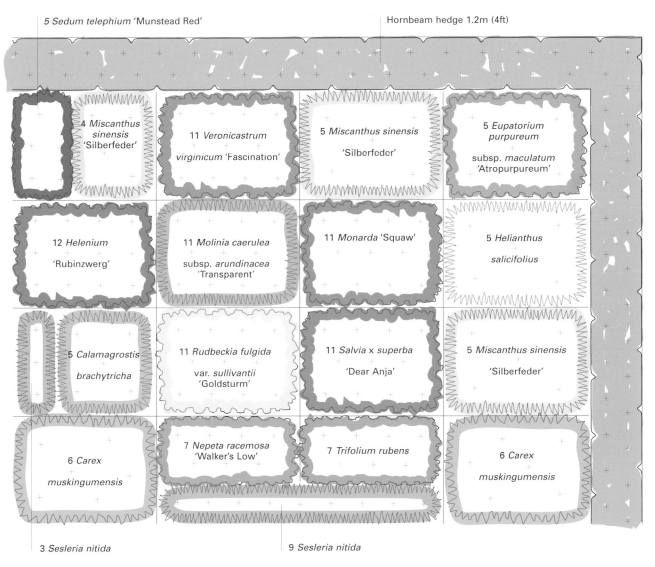

5 *Sedum telephium* 'Munstead Red'

Hornbeam hedge 1.2m (4ft)

4 *Miscanthus sinensis* 'Silberfeder'

11 *Veronicastrum virginicum* 'Fascination'

5 *Miscanthus sinensis* 'Silberfeder'

5 *Eupatorium purpureum* subsp. *maculatum* 'Atropurpureum'

12 *Helenium* 'Rubinzwerg'

11 *Molinia caerulea* subsp. *arundinacea* 'Transparent'

11 *Monarda* 'Squaw'

5 *Helianthus salicifolius*

5 *Calamagrostis brachytricha*

11 *Rudbeckia fulgida* var. *sullivantii* 'Goldsturm'

11 *Salvia x superba* 'Dear Anja'

5 *Miscanthus sinensis* 'Silberfeder'

6 *Carex muskingumensis*

7 *Nepeta racemosa* 'Walker's Low'

7 *Trifolium rubens*

6 *Carex muskingumensis*

3 *Sesleria nitida*

9 *Sesleria nitida*

minimalist planting plan

A brief for a minimalist, modern garden with strong clean lines and crisply cut hard landscape materials calls for a very restricted palette of plants that will enhance and not detract from the strength of the design (see pp.156–9). It is for an open sunny garden on free-draining soil of pH 6.5. Follow the various stages in Shady bed (see pp.118–19) through to completing the planting plan, tackling each planting area separately. The bed on one side of the path is to be 7.5m (24½ft) long by 1m (3ft) deep, while that opposite it is to be 7.5m (24½ft) long by 3m (10ft) deep.

Elevation and planting plan

BELOW AND BOTTOM On one side of the path, the mop-headed hornbeams (*Carpinus betulus*) are underplanted with evergreen ground cover *Pachysandra terminalis* and linked to the wall by a low box hedge. This is shown in 3D (below) and as a bird's eye view (bottom).

Combined planting plan

ABOVE RIGHT AND CENTRE RIGHT On the other side of the path, box hedges outline the geometric beds, where late spring colour is followed in summer by lavender and agapanthus. Both sides of the path appear on the planting plan: the new bed in detail (right centre), the other bed (right above) in outline only.

Sculptural effect

ABOVE In this modern garden a row of clipped hornbeam supplies a framework on either side of the garden. Beneath, two low hedges of box echo the lines of the rendered walls, reinforcing the strong crisp lines of the design.

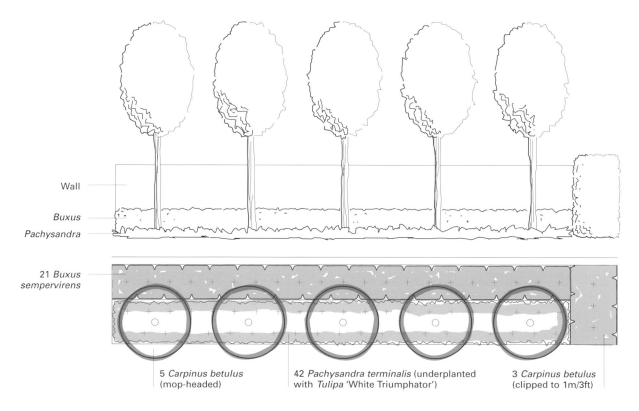

Wall

Buxus

Pachysandra

21 *Buxus sempervirens*

5 *Carpinus betulus* (mop-headed)

42 *Pachysandra terminalis* (underplanted with *Tulipa* 'White Triumphator')

3 *Carpinus betulus* (clipped to 1m/3ft)

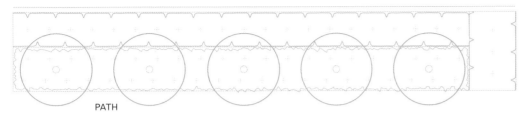

PATH

9 *Buxus*
(between each
block of planting)

12 *Lavandula angustifolia*
'Hidcote' (underplanted
with *Allium hollandicum*
'Purple Sensation')

12 *Lavandula angustifolia*
'Hidcote' (underplanted
with *Allium hollandicum*
'Purple Sensation')

9 *Carpinus
betulus*
(clipped to
1m/3ft)

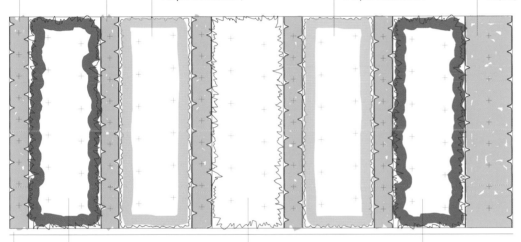

Wall 1m
(3ft) high

12 *Iris* 'Black Swan' (underplanted
with *Tulipa* 'White Triumphator')

12 *Agapanthus campanulatus*
var. *albidus*

12 *Iris* 'Black Swan'
(underplanted with *Tulipa*
'White Triumphator')

Late spring colour
LEFT Seasonal interest
will be provided by *Iris*
'Black Swan' (far left),
Allium hollandicum
'Purple Sensation' (left),
and *Tulipa* 'White
Triumphator'.

GIVING THE PLANTING PLAN
A PROFESSIONAL FINISH

If you are commissioned to do a planting plan for
someone else, you really do need to present it
attractively. Here are some tips on doing this:
- work on tracing paper fixed to your drawing board.
- place the plan and the elevation on the tracing paper.
- write a title across the top of the paper. Lettering can
  be word processed and then cut out and stuck onto the
  tracing paper with invisible tape covering all cut edges.
- in the bottom right-hand corner, include your contact
  information as well as details about the plan.

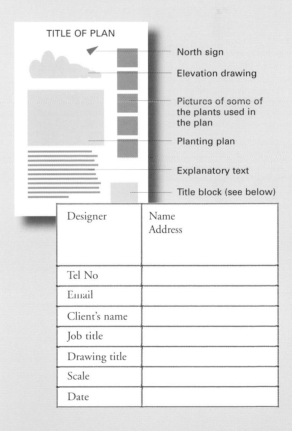

Designer	Name Address
Tel No	
Email	
Client's name	
Job title	
Drawing title	
Scale	
Date	

125

A garden can be designed in any style or theme so that there is no connection to or with the surrounding environment. This can work well in an urban setting, but in other areas the most successful gardens are generally those in which the surrounding landscape or architecture has influenced the design. The same is true for the planting. It is therefore important to follow the overall style or theme of a garden when developing the planting by selecting those plants that would grow naturally and so look most at home in that particular environment.

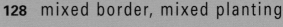

5 styles and themes

mixed border, mixed planting

The term mixed border does perhaps sound a little out of date so maybe mixed planting would be a better way of describing the type of planting that most people have in their gardens. This also depends on the size of the site and its location, because if you are planting up a town garden, or even a new garden in a more rural situation, then you will almost certainly be restricted by tight boundaries and most of the planted areas will be backed by a fence or, if you are lucky, a wall. The idea of mixed planting is that it should offer something of interest throughout the year, whether in the forms and textures of evergreen plants, coloured foliage, seasonal flowers, seedheads and fruits, autumn colour, or coloured stems.

The first stage in planning your planting is to analyse your site carefully, work out the aspect of each of the areas that are to be planted, and check the soil conditions. In most gardens you will have both sun and shade at different times of the day, so note which are your sunny and which are your shady areas and deal with each separately.

Then start to select your plants. If you are intending to plant a tree then choose this first. Begin at the back of the border and decide on your evergreen structural plants – remembering these should have fine or medium texture and that they need to be relatively fast growing. Most hollies, for example, are very slow growing so do not make good structural plants. Consider the form, texture, and leaf colour of each of the plants as well as any flowers or berries they may produce during the year. You can also use shade-tolerant climbers and wall shrubs at the back to provide seasonal interest, but do check their vigour. They can be tied to the wall or fence or be allowed to grow through the structural shrubs.

Once you have worked out the plants that will go along the back of the border consider where you need some specials or focal-point plants. Because of their distinctive qualities of, for example, strong form, coarse texture, or several seasons of interest, they will stand out from the other plants.

The next stage is the exciting part of the planting – your choice of shrubs and herbaceous plants for seasonal excitement and colour. In a large area you will have room for several deciduous shrubs that only have a short season of interest such as *Philadelphus* 'Belle Etoile', but in a small garden try to use those that also have interesting foliage as well as flowers. You may also select some plants just for their beautiful foliage such as *Cornus alba*

Structural evergreen plants
Back-of-border plants with fine or medium texture
Arbutus unedo
Choisya ternata
Cotoneaster salicifolius 'Rothschildianus'
Elaeagnus x ebbingei
Griselinia littoralis
Osmanthus x burkwoodii
Osmanthus heterophyllus
Photinia x *fraseri* 'Red Robin'
Pittosporum tenuifolium
Prunus lusitanica
Viburnum x burkwoodii
Viburnum tinus

'Sibirica Variegata' or that repeat-flower such as modern shrub roses. The range is seemingly endless, although you will always have your favourites.

A decision on herbaceous plants may be equally daunting, and it is best at first to keep to a limited range of reliable plants that you know, rather than picking and mixing from books. For the back of the border you will require some tall plants that have good flower form and preferably do not need staking: for example, *Anemone* × *hybrida* 'Honorine Jobert' and *Achillea filipendulina* 'Gold Plate'. For the middle and front of the planting

you should concentrate on some colourful plants. Limit the number of plants such as paeonies and poppies that flower for only a short time, and select those that give really good value. Penstemons start flowering in late spring and will continue right through until autumn, and *Sedum telephium* 'Purple Emperor' has deep purple foliage as well as long-lasting flowers.

It is important to ensure that the front and middle of the border look good even in the winter, so identify some small evergreen shrubs and herbaceous plants to support the ornamental planting.

When you have made your selection and finalized your basic planting plan you can then consider some bulbs to fill any gaps when the herbaceous plants die back. Go for the taller sturdier bulbs.

The plant lists on this and the following pages, although by no means comprehensive, might help you compile your own planting plans.

Evergreen structure
LEFT *Elaeagnus* x *ebbingei* defines the garden space and provides a backdrop for the more ornamental planting of herbaceous plants and grasses.

Supporting role
BELOW *Photinia* x *fraseri* 'Red Robin' enhances the rich array of flowering shrubs, climbing roses, and coloured foliage in this deep border.

Climbers and wall shrubs

Back-of-border plants with interesting foliage or flowers

Clematis alpina

Clematis viticella

Cotoneaster salicifolius 'Rothschildianus'

Garrya elliptica

Itea ilicifolia

Rhamnus alaternus 'Argenteovariegata'

Solanum laxum 'Album'

Trachelospermum jasminoides

Vitis amurensis

Vitis vinifera 'Purpurea'

Specials or focal-point plants

For an eye-catching accent in the border

Acer palmatum 'Sango-kaku'

Buxus sempervirens – clipped into spheres or cubes

Catalpa bignonioides 'Aurea' – pruned regularly

Cercis canadensis 'Forest Pansy'

Eriobotrya japonica

Euphorbia characias

Fatsia japonica – for shade

Mahonia x *media* 'Charity'

Nandina domestica

Phormium tenax

Ornamental shrubs

For creating seasonal change and excitement

Abelia x *grandiflora*

Buddleja davidii cvs

Choisya ternata 'Sundance'

Cistus x *purpureus*

Hebe 'Midsummer Beauty'

Hydrangea quercifolia

Philadelphus coronarius 'Variegatus'

Sambucus nigra 'Eva'

Viburnum x *burkwoodii*

Weigela 'Florida Variegata'

Front-of-border herbaceous plants

Low-growing plants with interesting foliage

Alchemilla mollis

Bergenia cvs

Brunnera macrophylla 'Hadspen Cream'

Epimedium sp. and cvs – for shade

Euphorbia amygdaloides var. *robbiae*

Geranium sp. and cvs

Heuchera cv

Lamium maculatum 'White Nancy'

Origanum vulgare 'Aureum'

Tellima grandiflora

Evergreen shrubs under 1m (3ft) high

For midborder structure and winter interest

Buxus sempervirens 'Suffruticosa'

Euonymus fortunei 'Emerald Gaiety'

Hebe 'Mrs Winder'

Pittosporum tenuifolium 'Tom Thumb'

Pittosporum tobira 'Nanum'

Prunus laurocerasus 'Zabeliana'

Sarcococca confusa

Skimmia x *confusa* 'Kew Green'

Viburnum davidii

Bulbs for mixed plantings

For filling gaps and extending the seasons

Allium cristophii

Allium giganteum

Allium hollandicum 'Purple Sensation'

Allium sphaerocephalon

Camassia sp.

Crocosmia cvs

Narcissus 'February Gold'

Narcissus 'Thalia'

Tulipa – the tall later flowering varieties

Strong forms

LEFT Clipped box (*Buxus*) is used to attract attention and so reinforce paths and entrances.

Late-season colour

ABOVE RIGHT In autumn the evening sun highlights seedheads and golden grasses.

Different greens

BELOW RIGHT The lime-green flowers of *Euphorbia characias* and *Alchemilla mollis* stand out against the variety of green forms and textures.

traditional herbaceous border

The traditional herbaceous border is probably only seen these days in a handful of large gardens in any country. While very beautiful they require a great deal of maintenance and have nothing of interest to offer in the winter months. There is no reason, however, why you should not create an herbaceous border on a smaller scale, or an island bed where you view the planting from all sides. Most herbaceous plants require an open sunny site and good soil with plenty of organic matter dug in. You then need to decide on an approach to the planting. Consider whether you are going to have a colour scheme, and if so whether it will be harmonious or contrasting (see pp.22–31). Then think about flowering times: will the border be at its best for just a few weeks or will it have interest throughout the summer months?

Once you have settled on the style of border, you can begin to plan it. Design your planting in drifts, starting with the taller plants at the back for a border, or along the centre for an island bed. Bear in mind that some tall plants need staking, which will increase maintenance. Consider the many different flower forms of herbaceous plants (see pp.14–15). You could put together some spikes and spires of different heights, for example, or you could contrast the spikes with buttons and globes, as well as a soft curtain or screening plant. The combinations are endless, and it is often difficult to get it right at the first attempt. Do take photographs and make notes during the first year, so that you have a record of groups that work or changes that you want to make at the end of the growing season.

There are numerous cultivars of herbaceous perennials, and it is best to work with a reliable nursery catalogue when making your decisions. The following lists of known reliable plants are just a starting point for your selection process.

Spires and spikes	Buttons and spheres		Umbels
Vertical flowers that add height and lift to the border	**For concentrated clusters of flowers and colour**		**For gently rounded forms like upturned bowls**
Aconitum sp. and cvs	*Astrantia major* 'Roma'		*Achillea filipendulina* 'Parker's Variety'
Actaea simplex	*Cirsium rivulare*		*Achillea* 'Terracotta'
Delphinium hybrids	*Echinops bannaticus* 'Taplow Blue'		*Anthriscus sylvestris* 'Ravenswing'
Lythrum virgatum cvs	*Eryngium bourgatii*		*Eupatorium purpureum* 'Atropurpureum'
Penstemon cvs	*Monarda* cvs		*Foeniculum vulgare* 'Purpureum'
Persicaria amplexicaulis 'Rosea'	*Phlox paniculata* cvs		*Lychnis chalcedonica* var. *albiflora*
Salvia nemorosa cvs	*Rudbeckia fulgida*		*Sedum telephium* 'Matrona'
Sanguisorba menziesii	*Rudbeckia occidentalis*		
Veronicastrum virginicum	*Trifolium rubens*		

Plumes

For soft forms creating a light fluffy effect

Amsonia hubrichtii

Astilbe thunbergii cvs

Calamagrostis brachytricha

Filipendula sp.

Gillenia trifoliata

Miscanthus sp. and cvs

Persicaria polymorpha

Thalictrum sp. and cvs

Screens and curtains

For airy transparent flowers that can be seen through

Crambe cordifolia

Foeniculum vulgare 'Giant Bronze'

Miscanthus sp. and cvs

Molinia caerulea 'Transparent'

Stipa gigantea

Thalictrum sp. and cvs

Verbena bonariensis

Daisy-like flower heads

For open sunny flowers with strong centres

Anthemis tinctoria cvs

Aster sp. and cvs

Helenium cvs

Helianthus salicifolius

Inula magnifica

Rudbeckia sp. and cvs

Unclassified plants for a herbaceous border

For very useful herbaceous plants that do not fit easily into any particular category

Alchemilla mollis

Anemone x *hybrida* cvs

Geranium sp. and cvs

Hemerocallis sp. and cvs

Heuchera cvs

Paeonia sp.

Papaver orientale cvs

Succession of flower forms

FAR LEFT Spikes, umbels, and buttons appear in early summer, while daisies, plumes, and screens will continue the display.

Traditional herbaceous border

LEFT This is backed by a hedge, has the tall plants at the back, and may include a mowing strip along the front.

new-wave, naturalistic planting

This is a much more informal way of using herbaceous plants and tends not to sit very happily with neatly mown lawns or small town gardens. Space is needed to create the exotic meadows of new-wave, naturalistic planting, which can then be combined with mown paths or gravel. Evergreen structure provided by clipped yew introduces a sense of order into this otherwise loose planting style. The numerous articles and books on this topic are an invaluable source of reference, as are visits to some of the planting schemes that have been created over the last few years.

The ecological approach of new-wave planting means that only those plants that thrive in the particular growing conditions are chosen. A moisture-retentive but free-draining soil and an open sunny site are required for this type of planting. Herbaceous plants generally do not do well on clay: they rot off in winter, get eaten by slugs and snails in spring, and wilt during a hot summer. When deciding on your plants try to restrict the number of different species in the same way that nature does in a wild flower meadow.

Plant in drifts of colour, and use grasses to create a matrix of green, which then becomes a soft gold later in the year. Bulbs too can add a touch of seasonal drama at different times of year – alliums being particularly effective. Choose only those plants that have a long flowering season and look good if left to stand during the winter months; they should also be able to survive competition from each other, not become invasive, not flop, and not be prolific seeders.

If you get all this right you will have a wonderfully successful planting scheme. There are endless plants to choose from, and the following are just a few suggestions for you to try and will complement the lists of herbaceous plants (see pp.132–3).

Naturalistic grasses

Foliage, flowers, and seedheads with contrasting forms and textures

Anemanthele lessoniana

Calamagrostis x *acutiflora*

Calamagrostis brachytricha

Deschampsia cespitosa

Miscanthus sinensis cvs

Molinia caerulea

Panicum virgatum cvs

Stipa calamagrostis

Stipa gigantea

Perfect plumes

ABOVE The tall plumes of a *Filipendula purpurea* cultivar supply the perfect foil for other herbaceous plants and grasses in Piet Oudolf's own garden.

The natural look

LEFT Grasses and herbaceous flowers and seedheads create a truly naturalistic effect in the borders at Bury Court, in Surrey, UK.

Attracting bees and butterflies

RIGHT *Monarda* 'Scorpion' with its vivid globe flowers is – like all the monarda cultivars – much loved by insects.

Winter wonders

Seedheads that last, and provide winter interest

Achillea cvs

Anemanthele lessoniana

Calamagrostis brachytricha

Digitalis ferruginea

Echinacea sp. and cvs

Eryngium sp.

Eupatorium purpureum 'Atropurpureum'

Miscanthus sinensis sp. and cvs

Phlomis sp.

Rudbeckia occidentalis and other sp.

Sedum cvs

Stipa gigantea

Verbena bonariensis

Veronicastrum virginicum

Naturalistic bulbs

Tough species that will seed and naturalize

Allium cristophii

Allium hollandicum

Allium karataviense

Allium sphaerocephalon

Camassia sp.

Fritillaria persica

Nectaroscordum siculum

dry, Mediterranean planting

For those who struggle to garden on cold wet clay it must be wonderful to have a light, free-draining soil and an open, sunny aspect where you can grow all those plants that come from the warmer regions of the world, such as the Mediterranean and South Africa. For many of these plants it is not so much the cold, as having their roots and stems in wet soil that is the real killer. If the soil is very dry it is a good idea to dig in some well-rotted organic matter when preparing the beds, in order to help the plants establish and to survive any drought conditions in future years. Many of these plants have adapted to a hot climate in various ways. Their leaves may be grey or silver, reduced in size, or rolled, felted or hairy; some may have waxy shiny surfaces, while others produce aromatic oils. Many develop deep tap roots to seek out available water, or they have underground storage organs such as bulbs or rhizomes, which enable them to survive underground. Plants with strong spiky forms such as yuccas, astelias, cordylines, and grasses as well as the pencil-like form of Italian cypress all look very at home in a Mediterranean-style planting. The colours will also be more vibrant than those found in more temperate native plants. As with the naturalistic planting (see pp.134–5) the seedheads of grasses and herbaceous plants can be left on to provide interest during winter.

Planting can be very informal with loose drifts of herbaceous plants, grasses, and ground cover, while shrubs and trees provide height and structure. Seedlings can be left to grow between established plants. Apply a mulch of gravel once planting is complete, because this will conserve moisture and also help to prevent weed growth.

Structural shrubs 1m (3ft) or more high

For small leaves or silver/grey foliage

Abelia x grandiflora

Atriplex halimus

Berberis x ottawensis f. purpurea 'Superba'

Brachyglottis Dunedin Group 'Sunshine'

Bupleurum fruticosum

Cistus sp.

Euphorbia mellifera

Nandina domestica

Phlomis fruticosa

Phormium cvs

Pittosporum tenuifolium

Pittosporum tobira

Rosa glauca

Rosa spinosissima

Trees for dry sites

Those that grow happily in hot dry conditions

Amelanchier lamarckii

Eucalyptus dalrympleana

Fraxinus angustifolia 'Raywood'

Genista aetnensis

Juniperus scopulorum 'Skyrocket'

Koelreuteria paniculata

Newly planted scree bed

RIGHT This extensive bed has been constructed out of gravel and railway sleepers and then planted with thymes, thrift, and *Salvia argentea*.

The perfect olive grove

FAR LEFT The trees in this grove are underplanted with *Iris germanica* and feather grass (*Stipa tenuissima*), while a rosemary flourishes in the foreground.

Invaluable self-seeders

LEFT At Hyde Hall, in Essex, UK, California poppy (*Eschscholzia californica*) self-seeds among other plants in the Gravel Garden.

Structural shrubs below 1m (3ft)

For tough plants with year-round structure and colour

Artemisia 'Powis Castle'

Astelia chathamica

Ballota sp.

Ceratostigma willmottianum

Cistus sp.

Cytisus x praecox cvs

Euphorbia characias

Hebe sp. and cvs

Helianthemum cvs

Lavandula pedunculata subsp. pedunculata

Parahebe perfoliata

Perovskia 'Blue Spire'

Phlomis italica

Pittosporum tenuifolium 'Tom Thumb'

Pittosporum tobira 'Nanum'

Salvia sp. and cvs

Santolina chamaecyparissus

Santolina rosmarinifolia

Yucca gloriosa

Perfumed planting

LEFT In the warm Mediterranean sun drifts of lavender provide an aromatic walkway to a pergola.

137

Mediterranean mood

ABOVE The walls set the mood for this planting in which spires of Jacob's rod (*Asphodeline lutea*) provide height amid early colour of *Iris* 'Black Swan', *Tulipa sprengeri*, rock roses (*Helianthemum* and *Cistus* x *skanbergii*), and thrift.

A hot dry habitat

ABOVE RIGHT Rocks and gravel are perfect for Mediterranean plants.

Reflecting the landscape

RIGHT Young pine trees here echo older pines visible in the landscape beyond.

Herbaceous plants for dry sites

For seasonal colour and excitement in hot dry conditions

Agapanthus sp. and cvs

Alstroemeria sp. and cvs

Anthemis sp. and cvs

Asphodeline sp.

Crambe cordifolia

Crambe maritima

Crocosmia sp. and cvs

Cynara cardunculus

Ferula communis

Galactites tomentosa

Libertia grandiflora

Libertia peregrinans

Nepeta racemosa 'Walker's Low'

Onopordum acanthium

Papaver cvs

Verbascum bombyciferum – biennial

See also New-wave, naturalistic planting (p.135)

Annuals for dry sites

Hardy annuals that will self-seed

Cerinthe major

Eschscholzia californica

Nigella damascena

Low plants for dry sites

For grounding the taller plants and softening the edges of the planting

Artemisia schmidtiana

Cotula lineariloba

Euphorbia myrsinites

Euphorbia rigida

Glaucium flavum

Origanum sp. and cvs

Osteospermum ecklonis

Phlox sp. and cvs

Phuopsis stylosa

Stachys byzantina

Thymus cvs

Bulbs for dry sites

All require a good baking after flowering

Galtonia candicans

Gladiolus communis subsp. *byzantinus*

Iris germanica cvs

Iris unguicularis

Nerine bowdenii

Tulipa sp.

See also New-wave, naturalistic planting (p.135)

woodland, shade

Most people have some areas of shade in their garden, and many who live in towns and cities may have gardens that receive virtually no direct sunlight even in summer, because of high boundary walls or buildings. Others may have trees in their garden where the leaf canopy casts shade during summer but allows light in during winter and early spring before the leaves are out. Planting such areas may seem a little problematical at first, but if you accept that these areas are like woodland and you copy the way that nature deals with them then you should enjoy success. Dry shade, however, particularly in an area that receives virtually no rain or light and is full of dense fibrous tree roots, can be almost impossible to plant.

When selecting plants for shade you need to accept that green will be the predominant colour. Most of the bulbs and herbaceous plants used in sunnier parts of the garden will not survive in shade. Flowering shrubs will become drawn and leggy as they seek out the light.

The leaves of shade-loving plants will often be dark green, large, and sometimes shiny – all of which improve the ability to photosynthesize. Most shade-loving plants flower early in the year, before the leaf canopy is out, so that they receive the maximum amount of light and are then green for the rest of the year or in the case of bulbs disappear altogether.

The approach to planting up a shady or woodland area can vary. In established woodland, in a rural situation, it may be most effective to plant natives such as drifts of wood anemones and bluebells, supported by the textures of ferns, mosses, and ivies. Alternatively you could introduce more ornamental plants that can be used in a greater variety of shady situations. It should also be remembered that it takes many years for a newly planted tree to cast real shade, so it is inappropriate to plant shade-lovers until the tree is really established. The light levels within a woodland will also vary, because some areas on the margins will receive direct light while others farther in will be in deep shade once the tree canopy is fully out. The listed plants are suitable for full or partial shade. Although most ferns will also be happy in such a situation, they have not been included here.

Shrubs for heavy shade
For evergreen foliage and early flowering
Buxus sempervirens
Danae racemosa
Mahonia aquifolium 'Apollo'
Mahonia x *media* 'Charity'
Prunus laurocerasus 'Otto Luyken'
Prunus laurocerasus 'Zabeliana'
Prunus lusitanica
Sarcococca confusa
Skimmia x *confusa* 'Kew Green'
Skimmia japonica 'Kew White'
Skimmia laureola
Viburnum davidii
Viburnum rhytidophyllum
Viburnum tinus

Riverbank planting
FAR LEFT The sides of this stream have been sympathetically planted with hostas and ferns to create a woodland floor.

Ornamental woodland
LEFT Woodland species such as bergenias, forget-me-nots (*Myosotis*), and *Skimmia* x *confusa* 'Kew Green' thrive under the canopy of mature oak trees.

The jungle-like effect
RIGHT The tree fern *Dicksonia antarctica*, *Gunnera manicata*, and coloured hosta leaves all contribute to this shady, lush area.

Herbaceous plants for shade

All require moist soil and some shade

Actaea simplex

Anemone x *hybrida* cvs

Aquilegia sp.

Aruncus dioicus

Astrantia major cvs

Dicentra spectabilis 'Alba'

Digitalis sp.

Euphorbia schillingii

Maianthemum racemosum

Paeonia mlokosewitschii

Polygonatum x *hybridum*

Rodgersia aesculifolia

Thalictrum sp.

Uvularia grandiflora

Wide array

RIGHT Woodland and shade-loving plants are very varied.

1 *Onoclea sensibilis*
2 *Maianthemum racemosum*
3 *Arum italicum* berries
4 *Cornus mas*
5 *Euphorbia amygdaloides* var. *robbiae*
6 *Digitalis purpurea* f. *albiflora*
7 *Pulmonaria* 'Beth's Pink'
8 *Aquilegia vulgaris* 'Nivea'
9 *Tellima grandiflora* Rubra Group

7

8

6

9

Large structural shrubs for shade

For height and interest from foliage, flowers, or fruit

Acer palmatum cvs

Cornus mas cvs

Corylopsis sp. – requires acid soil

Deutzia sp.

Euonymus europaeus 'Red Cascade'

Hamamelis mollis

Hydrangea aspera Villosa Group

Hydrangea macrophylla cvs

Ilex aquifolium cvs

Kolkwitzia amabilis

Philadelphus coronarius 'Aureus'

Ribes laurifolium

Rubus 'Benenden'

Weigela 'Florida Variegata'

Shade-lovers

Grasses, sedges, and rushes that will grow in shade

Carex elata 'Aurea'

Carex oshimensis 'Evergold'

Deschampsia cespitosa

Hakonechloa macra 'Aureola'

Luzula nivea – for semi-shade

Luzula sylvatica cvs

Ground cover for shade

Low-growing plants with good flowers and interesting foliage

Ajuga reptans cvs

Alchemilla mollis

Arum italicum subsp. *italicum* 'Marmoratum'

Bergenia cvs

Brunnera macrophylla cvs

Dicentra formosa var. *alba*

Epimedium sp. and cvs

Euphorbia amygdaloides var. *robbiae*

Geranium sp. and cvs

Helleborus x *hybridus*

Heuchera cylindrica 'Greenfinch'

Hosta sp. and cvs

Lamium maculatum 'White Nancy'

Polemonium 'Lambrook Mauve'

Pulmonaria sp. and cvs

Ranunculus ficaria cvs

Tellima grandiflora

Viola riviniana Purpurea Group

143

cottage style

Ask someone to describe a cottage garden and they will probably picture a cottage in the country with roses round the door, butterflies and bees flitting from plant to plant, and fruit trees, herbaceous plants, annuals, and vegetables all growing in perfect harmony. Achieving this idyll is another matter, because this type of garden is very labour-intensive, and if left alone for even a short while soon becomes untidy and unproductive. If you do favour a cottage-garden style of planting, ensure that you keep the layout as simple as possible, avoid having a lawn if you can, and allow the plants to spill over onto informal gravel paths. It is also simpler to grow most of the fruit and vegetables in separate beds away from the flower borders, although you could use some decorative lettuce or herbs as edging plants and twine some runner beans and sweet peas up wigwams in the borders to create a real cottage-garden feel.

Plant selection needs to follow the same process as for any other style of planting. Begin by deciding on a tree. In a small garden with room for only one tree choose a fruit tree, and where space allows for more then select an ornamental tree such as an amelanchier, medlar (*Mespilus*), or a winter-flowering cherry. Your next decision should be on shrubs for height and structure and then look at herbaceous plants and bulbs. Many of the herbaceous plants such as lupins and delphiniums that were traditionally used in cottage gardens require staking and are over very early in the summer, so where possible think of more modern alternatives that can stand up on their own and also flower for longer. You could even include some grasses. Because old-fashioned roses usually have only one flush of flowers, you might prefer modern shrub roses that both repeat-flower and are more resistant to diseases.

Extra colour can be provided by letting annuals such as honesty, evening primroses, and poppies self-seed in the borders and by introducing seasonal bedding, which can be planted in containers.

Cottage plants

FAR LEFT Delphiniums, Jacob's ladder (*Polemonium*), and catmint (*Nepeta*) here enhance exuberant roses.

Modern look

LEFT Colourful furniture and tropical palms create a vibrant cottage-style garden.

Shrubs for the cottage garden

Reliable, "old-fashioned" plants with pretty flowers or good foliage

Buddleja davidii cvs

Buxus sempervirens

Choisya ternata

Corylus avellana

Hebe sp. and cvs

Hydrangea macrophylla cvs

Ilex aquifolium cvs

Philadelphus sp. and cvs

Ribes sanguineum White Icicle 'Ubric'

Rosa cvs

Spiraea 'Arguta'

Syringa vulgaris cvs

Viburnum x *burkwoodii*

Viburnum opulus 'Roseum'

Viburnum tinus

Weigela cvs

A potager

In this ornamental vegetable garden the beds are normally laid out in a formal geometric pattern, like a knot garden, and the whole garden is enclosed by a wall or hedge such as yew. The beds are edged with low hedges of clipped box, lavender, or santolina as well as herbs such as thyme, parsley, and chives. Fruit trees can be trained into fans, espaliers, cordons, or stepovers, and roses are grown over arches or used as standards in the beds. Herbaceous plants can be grown in separate borders around the edge.

Attractive potager
BELOW A mixture of flowers, herbs, and vegetables grow within the beds of this ornamental vegetable garden.

Eye-catching vegetable beds
RIGHT Wigwams support the decorative runner beans and at the back rhubarb leaves supply contrasting coarse texture.

Herbaceous plants

"Old-fashioned" flowers for colour, scent, and cutting

Aconitum sp. and cvs

Alcea sp.

Alchemilla mollis

Aquilegia sp. and cvs

Astrantia major cvs

Campanula sp.

Centranthus ruber

Cirsium rivulare 'Atropurpureum'

Delphinium cvs

Dianthus sp.

Digitalis sp.

Erigeron karvinskianus

Galium odoratum

Geranium sp. and cvs

Hesperis matronalis

Lupinus sp.

Lychnis coronaria cvs

Nepeta sp.

Paeonia sp.

Papaver orientale cvs

Penstemon cvs

Phlox sp.

Polemonium caeruleum

Sisyrinchium striatum

Stachys macrantha

Thalictrum aquilegiifolium

Climbers for the cottage garden

For height, colour, or scent in the border

Akebia quinata

Clematis sp.

Clematis 'Etoile Violette'

Clematis 'Purpurea Plena Elegans'

Clematis viticella cvs

Jasminum officinale

Lonicera pericylmenum 'Serotina'

Rosa 'Cécile Brunner'

Rosa 'Félicité Perpétue'

Rosa 'New Dawn'

Vitis vinifera 'Purpurea'

Wisteria sinensis

Shrub roses

For repeat-flowering through the summer

Rosa 'Blanche Double de Coubert'

Rosa Gertrude Jekyll

Rosa 'Penelope'

Rosa 'Roserie de l'Haÿ'

Any English shrub rose

meadows and biodiversity

Sustainability and biodiversity are two words that are heard very frequently these days, and there have been numerous articles on both in the gardening press. Sustainability relates more to design issues and carbon footprints, while biodiversity is very relevant to planting because it looks at how gardens and public spaces are used to sustain as wide a range of wildlife species as possible. Certain factors such as creating a natural pond, leaving seedheads on herbaceous perennials, and retaining berries and hips on shrubs and roses will all help to attract birds and small mammals into the garden. When selecting ornamental plants choose species that are rich in nectar and pollen such as buddleja, lavenders, hebes, and sedums, because these attract butterflies and bees into the garden. Bees are effective pollinators of fruit and vegetables, so are especially welcome in a productive garden.

Roadside verges are important nature reserves: other than for one seasonal cut, they are rarely disturbed so give shelter to a wide range of native flowers and wildlife. Some town councils are now planting up grass verges, roundabouts, and borders in parks with wild flower mixes in order to support biodiversity and also to reduce costs.

In the garden it may not be practical to plant a wild flower meadow but you could leave lawn weeds such as self-heal and speedwell to naturalize in one area, and this would encourage butterflies, moths, and other beneficial insects such as ladybirds and hoverflies into your garden. You could also create a wild area for spring with naturalized bulbs and wild flowers such as primroses and lady's smock, followed by cow parsley and campion. A true wild flower meadow is in reality quite difficult to both plant and maintain, and it is not an "easy option". If the land has been used for agriculture then it will be too nutrient-rich for most native flowers, which thrive on poor soils, and vigorous weeds such as dock and creeping thistle are likely to cause a problem.

Helpful hoverflies
ABOVE Many native plants such as teasels (*Dipsacus*), produce nectar and pollen for insects.

Beneficial ground cover
RIGHT Beneath the olive trees a golden meadow provides ground cover for wildlife and insects.

Roadside colour
FAR RIGHT Hardy annuals are an inexpensive and colourful way of enhancing grass verges.

Herbaceous plants to attract wildlife

Achillea sp.

Aster sp.

Centranthus sp.

Erigeron sp.

Helenium sp.

Scabiosa sp.

Sedum spectabile

Shrubs to attract bees and butterflies

Buddleja davidii

Buddleja globosa

Cotoneaster sp.

Lavandula sp.

Rhamnus sp.

Trees and shrubs to encourage birds

Arbutus unedo

Cotoneaster sp.

Ilex sp.

Malus sp.

Prunus avium

Pyracantha sp.

Rosa rugosa

Sambucus sp.

Viburnum opulus

water and bog

There are many different ways of using water in the garden, and it is important to establish the style of the water feature you prefer because this will influence the plant selection. Formal water features are usually geometric and incorporated into the hard landscaping close to the house or a sitting area. They are often designed to be reflective pools or may have a fountain as a focal point, and are best left unplanted. Informal pools on the other hand are usually more organic in shape, and are often designed to have sloping edges and perhaps a pebble beach. They fit well into areas of grass or gravel and provide the perfect environment for aquatic planting and wildlife. An informal water feature could also include a flowing stream or a waterfall. If you intend to introduce fish into a pool it is really important to plant up the pool first. This allows the plants to absorb the excess nutrients so that the water will clear as a balance is established. This may take a little while, so there is need for patience at this stage. When the fish are introduced the established plants will be able to utilize the extra nutrients that will be excreted by the fish, and this helps to prevent algal growth and the water turning green.

When planting up a pool keep the planting fairly simple, so that it enhances the surroundings and the water remains the main focus. If you do not know very much about aquatic plants it is worth seeking advice from a specialist supplier, because they will be able to give guidance on vigour and the most appropriate plants for different parts of the pool. Water plants fall into various categories depending on the depth of water they prefer.

Floating-leaved plants

This group of plants is important because they have leaves that float on the surface of the water, so blocking out sunlight and helping to prevent algal growth. They also provide shade and shelter for pond life. In order to grow successfully they require a minimum of 30cm (12in) of water.

Floating-leaved plants

For providing shelter and shade for wildlife

Aponogeton distachyos

Azolla filiculoides

Hydrocharis morsus-ranae

Nuphar japonica

Nymphaea cvs

Nymphoides peltata

Stratiotes aloides

Submerged oxygenators

Important for improving water quality

Ceratophyllum demersum

Hottonia palustris

Lagarosiphon major

Myriophyllum verticillatum

Potamogeton crispus

Ranunculus aquaticus

Water lilies are the most popular "floaters" but are not always suitable, because they can be quite invasive. They also generally require deeper water and will not tolerate moving water. Some deep-water plants are anchored by their roots in bottom soil or else are planted in plastic crates or baskets. Some floaters such as water soldier (*Pistia stratiotes*) tend to sink to the bottom of the pool in winter and rise back to the surface in spring.

Submerged oxygenators

It is really important to have a few oxygenating plants in the pool. They will compete with the algae for nutrients and release oxygen into the water, enabling it to support life. Most oxygenators are sold as bunches of cuttings fastened together with a strip of lead and are planted into baskets placed on the bottom of the pool.

Marginal and other moisture-lovers

Marginal plants are found near a pool and grow in mud or shallow water. Plant them in the depth of water that best suits each species. Their varied forms and textures help to soften the edge of the pool and provide cover for wildlife. They often grow quickly, so it is best to plant them in containers; this also protects any flexible pond liner from root damage.

Many other plants positively thrive in moist but not waterlogged soil. They include not only those plants seen growing naturally alongside water but also many normally grown in drier conditions such as hemerocallis that grow with greater lushness in moist soils. These plants are used to bridge the gap between the aquatic planting and the rest of the garden. Some suit a naturalistic planting style, while others are better in a more ornamental one, so you need to consider what you are trying to achieve.

Exotic feel
LEFT *Gunnera manicata* – a native of Brazil – thrives alongside the tree fern *Dicksonia antarctica* in this lush poolside planting.

Enhanced setting
RIGHT The planting around this pool includes the repeated use of loosestrife (*Lysimachia punctata*) with its bright yellow flowers and the varied textures of plants such as *Ligularia dentata* 'Desdemona', bamboos, and sedges.

Marginal plants

For softening the edge of the pool and providing a habitat for wildlife

Butomus umbellatus

Caltha palustris

Iris ensata cvs

Iris pseudacorus 'Variegata'

Menyanthes trifoliata

Mimulus luteus

Pontederia cordata

Ranunculus lingua 'Grandiflorus'

Zantedeschia aethiopica 'Crowborough'

Moisture-loving plants

Ornamental plants that enjoy the poolside habitat

Actaea simplex

Angelica archangelica

Aruncus dioicus

Astilbe cvs

Carex elata 'Aurea'

Cornus sericea 'Flaviramea'

Darmera peltata

Filipendula sp. and cvs

Gunnera manicata

Hemerocallis fulva

Hosta sp. and cvs

Iris sibirica cvs

Ligularia sp. and cvs

Lysimachia nummularia 'Aurea'

Lysimachia punctata

Miscanthus sinensis 'Zebrinus'

Osmunda regalis

Persicaria bistorta 'Superba'

Petasites japonicus

Primula sp. and cvs

Rheum sp.

Rodgersia sp.

Veratrum album

"Watery" plants

RIGHT There exists an array of aquatic and marginal plants.

1 *Orontium aquaticum*
2 *Butomus umbellatus*
3 *Pontederia cordata*
4 *Gunnera manicata*
5 *Darmera peltata*
6 *Hemerocallis dumortieri*
7 *Aruncus dioicus*
8 *Nymphaea* 'Pink Sensation'
9 *Iris pseudacorus*
10 *Menyanthes trifoliata*
11 *Hosta* 'Frances Williams'
12 *Rodgersia podophylla*

minimalist, modern

The characteristics of a modern-style garden are simplicity of line coupled with smooth, crisply cut materials, giving the space an almost sculptural quality. The shapes can be either geometric or organic, and the planting also needs to be simple and uncluttered so that the whole garden functions as an outdoor living space. Minimalist planting is usually low maintenance and well suited to people who have no gardening knowledge or skills. The plant selection is quite restricted, and because most of the plants are evergreen maintenance consists of clipping or thinning out rather than skilful pruning.

The colours used for the materials and accessories are usually muted greys, silvers, and buffs, and the plants themselves are selected for their strong sculptural forms and varied textures in tints, tones, and shades of green that will support the design all year. Clipped box spheres and cubes are often used to provide a framework for large sculptural plants such as tree ferns, bamboos, pleached or multistemmed trees, and grasses. Ground cover may be simple: for example, clipped ivy, a low-growing bamboo, or a layer of pebbles that blend with the materials used for the hard landscaping. A single plant or several small plants of the same species can be grown in containers and placed in lines or groups to echo the design and hard landscaping. In a larger space, for example around a swimming pool, a minimalist design can work well when planted up using herbaceous plants and grasses in the new-wave, naturalistic style (see pp.134–5).

Verdant scene

FAR RIGHT A generous green backdrop provides the setting for this stylish pool, where clipped hedges of *Elaeagnus* x *ebbingei* and the arching form of a cultivar of *Miscanthus sinensis* soften the outline of the pool.

Sculptural forms

RIGHT These tall containers, which are reflected in the pool, have been simply planted with *Phormium* 'Bronze Baby'. The phormiums echo the colour of the containers, making a bold statement alongside the pool.

Pleached trees

For providing strong form and structure

Carpinus betulus

Pyrus calleryana 'Chanticleer'

Tilia cordata

Sculptural trees

For eye-catching or architectural interest

Acer griseum

Betula albosinensis var. *septentrionalis*

Betula utilis var. *jacquemontii*

Cupressus sempervirens Stricta Group

Dicksonia antarctica

Eriobotrya japonica

Eucalyptus pauciflora subsp. *niphophila*

Pinus mugo

Pinus pinea

Bamboos for a modern garden

Thin out culms for a sculptural effect

Chusquea culeou

Phyllostachys aurea

Phyllostachys nigra

Ground cover for a modern garden

Plants with carpeting habits or strong forms

Hedera helix cvs

Hosta sieboldiana

Ophiopogon planiscapus 'Nigrescens'

Polypodium sp. and cvs

Polystichum sp. and cvs

Plants for containers

Sculptural forms to complement modern materials

Buxus – spheres and cubes

Hebe 'Emerald Gem'

Laurus nobilis – clipped

Olea europaea

Pittosporum tobira 'Nanum'

Taxus baccata – clipped

Bold shapes

LEFT Agaves provide a stunning contrast in colour and form with the bold blue and terracotta walls behind.

Pristine lines

BELOW LEFT Neatly clipped box *(Buxus)* hedging repeats the shapes of the walls, giving the area a very manicured feel.

Reinforcing an axis

BELOW RIGHT In a New Zealand garden the silvery leaves of a coprosma hedge reflect the colour of the metal grid.

Oriental theme

RIGHT The use of Japanese style and plants, as here, can also create a minimalist effect.

Alternative to grass

FAR RIGHT *Selliera radicans* softens the paving around this angular pool.

exotics

People tend to notice exotic plants because generally they look out of place among softer green plantings. With temperate winters becoming warmer, however, more of these strongly architectural plants such as palms and tree ferns are being used in towns and cities in which frosts are almost a thing of the past. According to the dictionary, "exotic" means originating from a foreign country or something that is strikingly colourful and unusual. An exotic plant therefore is one that has bold and distinctive foliage, it may have brightly coloured flowers or foliage, and could well need protection during winter. Exotics fit best with the clean lines of modern or minimalist architecture usually found in towns and cities. They look totally out of place in a more rural setting. Because towns and cities are warmer than the surrounding countryside, they offer greater shelter and protection to plants during winter.

Many exotics have large spiky leaves, and these plants also associate effectively with rock and gravel, suggesting more desert-like conditions. As most exotics have strong forms or coarse texture they immediately demand attention. Therefore planting too many in a confined space can make it very claustrophobic. Some plants such as agaves and bananas will probably need some winter protection, and they can either be left outside and wrapped in fleece or be moved into a glasshouse for winter.

When using exotics it is best to group several plants together so that they make a strong visual impact. Then leave a large amount of space around the group except for introducing very simple, fine- or medium-textured ground cover plants. These ground cover plants will provide an invaluable foil for the exotics, enhancing their star qualities and focusing attention on the grouping itself.

Excitement

LEFT Pampas grass (*Cortaderia*), banana palms (*Musa*), and castor oil plants (*Ricinus communis*) look truly exotic with hot-coloured dahlias and cannas.

Unusual companions

BELOW Foxtail lily (*Eremurus* x *isabellinus* Shelford hybrids) go well with roses.

Powerful lilies

RIGHT Lily flowers add a strong form and heavy scent to a bed or border.

Tropical blooms

FAR RIGHT Cannas, originating from tropical North and South America, create an exotic touch in any planting scheme.

Bold exotics

Plants that have a strong presence from size or colour

Agave americana

Cordyline australis

Cortaderia cvs

Dicksonia antarctica

Echium sp.

Eremurus hybrids

Gunnera manicata

Lagerstroemia indica cvs

Musa basjoo

Phormium tenax

Strelitzia reginae

Trachycarpus fortunei

Washingtonia robusta

Yucca filamentosa

Less dramatic exotics

These need to be planted in groups for maximum impact

Agapanthus sp. and cvs

Allium giganteum

Amaryllis belladonna

Canna indica cvs

Crinum x *powellii*

Dahlia cvs

Kniphofia cvs

Ricinus communis

161

containers

Plants grown in containers present an effective method of cultivation in difficult or impossible situations such as balconies, forecourts, streets, courtyards, patios, or suspended from buildings and lamp-posts. They are also very useful in providing continuous interest, because pots can be replaced by others as soon as they fade or they can be planted up with shrubs or small trees to provide all-year structure and interest in an otherwise dull area.

The choice of container is very important: the style and materials should be in keeping with the overall style of the garden. Terracotta seems to fit almost any situation, while a galvanized metal container planted up with the sharp form of a yucca or a clipped box cube suggests a more modern style. It is also important to get the scale of the containers right. Often what looks fairly large at the garden centre can, once home, become lost on an empty patio or be completely dwarfed by the size of the building. Containers look best when grouped together, but avoid using too many small pots. Always stand back when grouping and planting up your pots, and view them with the building behind to make sure that the scale of both pots and plants is right for the situation.

Planting containers with seasonal bedding in autumn (for spring colour) and again in late spring (for summer colour) can be very expensive, so it is a good idea to use permanent planting such as a small tree, evergreen shrubs, or herbaceous plants in some containers and then to introduce seasonal colour in just a few containers. Avoid a dotty effect with your planting. One pot planted up with several of the same species will have far greater impact than one with a mix of plants. In a group of pots think about forms, textures, and colour, as you would if planting in the garden.

Selecting the right compost is also important if your plants are to flourish. Peat-based potting compost is light and easy to handle but dries out very quickly and is low on nutrients. A loam-based one is easier to manage and is particularly suitable for larger plants, because it contains more nutrients and is heavier. The pots therefore are less likely to blow over on a windy day. A good compromise – particularly for short-lived plants – can be to make up a mix of the two potting compost types. Containers with permanent planting can be mulched with pebbles or gravel, to help conserve moisture and to provide a decorative finish.

Mediterranean atmosphere

LEFT These stylish Italianate containers defining the edge of the terrace are planted with citrus trees bearing miniature oranges.

Mystical mood

ABOVE Spiders have threaded their gossamer webs over the pot-grown agaves one early autumn morning.

Modern metal

RIGHT Crisply clipped box (*Buxus*) squares make the ideal planting material in these galvanized containers.

Herbaceous plants, grasses etc

Can be planted with trees and shrubs to extend interest

Agapanthus sp. and cvs

Hakonechloa macra cvs

Hedera cvs

Herbs

Libertia grandiflora

Polypodium sp. and cvs

Polystichum sp. and cvs

Sempervivum cvs

Seasonal planting – spring

For planting out in autumn to provide spring colour

Bellis perennis

Narcissus cvs

Tulipa cvs

Viola cvs

Seasonal planting – summer

For planting out at the end of spring

Aeonium 'Zwartkop'

Argyranthemum sp. and cvs

Echeveria

Lilium cvs

Pelargonium 'Black Knight'

Pelargonium 'Lord Bute'

Endless opportunities

RIGHT Innumerable styles and themes can be displayed in pots and other containers.

1 Minimalism on a modern roof garden
2 Traditional Versailles container
3 A staged display of succulents
4 Spiky blue fescue (*Festuca glauca*) in smooth concrete
5 Hebes make ideal subjects for containers
6 Houseleeks (*Sempervivum*) provide a rich tapestry of different textures
7 Sculptural effect from box (*Buxus*) and container
8 The strong forms of box spheres are surrounded by coarse textures
9 Summer colour from verbena and trailing ivy
10 Box ball reflects shape of hydrangea flowers
11 Containers used as small pools on the patio

Those of you who have successfully designed or planted up your own garden might well find that friends or family call on you to give advice and help them plant their own gardens. This could well start you thinking about how you might turn your talents into running a small business. Many people start by doing some gardening and planting in their own locality, and then, finding that they need a greater range of skills and knowledge, sign up for a recognized gardening or design course at a local college. This section of the book explains more about running a garden design business such as legal considerations, plant buying, and costing a job. These general guidelines will help you find your own way of working as a garden designer and dealing professionally with clients, friends, and family.

6 aspects of business

designing for others

Before acquiring your first client you need to spend some time creating a professional image for your business. This will include organizing items of stationery such as business cards, headed notepaper, and leaflets setting out the services you offer. It is also helpful to put together a small portfolio showing a variety of gardens and planting schemes, because this will be useful when you are talking to a client, trying to establish their requirements. You also need to think about charges and how you are going to keep a detailed record of each project and how long it takes.

When a client contacts you, you need to arrange a visit. Most designers charge an hourly rate for this. Keep this initial meeting fairly brief: show the client your portfolio of drawings and pictures but do not give too much away. It is very useful to have a checklist to use at this first visit. This will ensure that you cover all the relevant topics such as family members and pets, current problems with planting, specific requirements such as foliage or flowers for cutting, the client's plant knowledge and skills, and time available for maintenance. Such a checklist will also remind you to check soil type and its pH (see pp.96–7) and the aspect of the site (see pp.94–5). If the client likes the sort of work you do and wants to employ you, you can then arrange a further visit of a more exploratory nature, in which to discuss ideas more fully. Often clients will not be very clear about what they do want, so you should take the lead on this.

If the site has been designed quite recently, then plans should be available for you to work from, although it is still worth checking a few measurements for accuracy. Where there are no up-to-date plans, you will have to measure up the areas yourself. Accompany the measurements with a quick sketch plan and take lots of photographs, which you can refer to later. Before leaving the site, ensure that you have all the information you require, because the next stage in the process will be drawing up the client brief and working out the cost of creating a planting plan.

SITE AND CLIENT CHECKLIST

Create a checklist template on your computer and take a copy with you when you visit a client.

Examples of questions to ask
- name and address
- location, style, and materials of house
- family, children, pets
- gardening knowledge/interests
- aspect of garden
- soil type and pH
- problems with planting identified by client
- trees and plants client would like to retain
- favourite plants and colours
- planting requirements
- level of maintenance
- client budget

Wide-ranging views
ABOVE Try to involve not only the commissioning client but also other family members when discussing changes.

Design aids
LEFT Collect a range of photographs that show different styles of planting and use them in a portfolio or concept (mood) board to help a client visualize the style of planting they might like.

SITE AND CLIENT CHECKLIST

Name	Mr and Mrs Smith – Peter and Sarah
Address	Jasmine Cottage, Hoe Lane, Wickam

Location, style, and materials of house

In the centre of a small village, quiet lane, little traffic. Lovely views from garden out across the hills. Detached 19th-century cottage. Brown/red flecked brick. slate roof. Paintwork is soft blue /grey. Traditional furniture – pine but cottage has modern feel inside.

Family, children, pets

the client brief

Following your visit to the client you should review all the notes, sketches, measurements, and photographs taken during the meeting so you can produce a client brief. This is a very important document, because it will set out for the client your understanding of their wishes and requirements. Once the brief has been agreed by the client you must keep to it and not make any changes without first consulting the client. It is best not to start work on any project until the client has signed a copy of the brief, which then takes the form of a contract. If they do require changes at a later date, then you can charge for the extra work. If, however, you make changes without consulting them it could jeopardize your final payment. When you send the client the brief you can also set out your charges for the project (see pp.184–5). If you are doing a planting plan you should state the cost of the plan and also mention that in order to proceed with the work you require 50 percent of the cost at once and the rest when you present the actual plan to them.

Report writing

The ability to write a highly readable professional report is an invaluable skill to acquire. You may need to write a report for several reasons.

Firstly it may be that a client has commissioned you to look at their garden and advise them on how it might be improved. In this case you can write up your findings in the form of a report, and include sketches, plant lists, and as much information as needed.

Secondly you may be asked to present ideas in writing, perhaps to a committee, when they are approaching more than one person about a particular job. The report in this instance will probably be the deciding factor as to whether or not you get the job.

Thirdly you may need to write a report to accompany a plan, outlining a scheme in greater detail. There may also be details that should be

Checking the details

ABOVE Before leaving the site ensure that you have all the information and details you need to write the brief and complete the design for your client.

explained more fully for future maintenance, such as the height of hedges or planting schemes for containers.

Structure of a report

Front cover A report must have a professional front cover or title page, and this must impress the client before they have even opened the document. It should state:

- the title of the report
- who the report is for, that is the client's name and address
- the designer's details, that is your name, address, phone number, and email address;
- date of the report

Contents page This will list all the headings and subheadings within the report and the appropriate page numbers.

Introduction This should be the first paragraph in the report. It should give the general background to the report as well as its scope, and could include details such as where the site is located and why the report has been commissioned.

Main body of the report The structure of the report will be dictated by what you have to say. Let logic dictate its order, so review the current situation first and then make recommendations for change. Always remember who you are writing the report for; it needs to be interesting, stimulating, and visually exciting with a "wow factor". If your report is dull then your work will probably be dull too. Other factors to bear in mind are:

- use numbered headings and subheadings in bold, and insert illustrations wherever appropriate, in order to avoid long pages of text
- write in the third person: "the site was surveyed…", "it is suggested…", rather than "I surveyed the site…" or "I suggest…"
- be generous with space. The impact of a well-designed layout is immense, so use double spacing between the lines of text
- align all text and illustrations to the left side of the page, and do not indent paragraphs

Conclusion or summary Always end your report with a short conclusion that briefly draws together all the information you have presented in your report. Do not introduce any new material at this stage.

Presenting your report Your report must be printed and placed in a document cover.

CLIENT BRIEF

After the initial meeting with the client and before doing any work, it is really important that the designer sets out his or her understanding of the client's requirements. A copy of this client brief then needs to be signed by the client.

Examples of client requirements

- retain the two existing apple trees in back garden
- arrange for remedial work to be carried out on both trees
- retain mature *Viburnum tinus* and *Prunus lusitanica* in border on right side of garden
- clear all other planting
- style of planting to be fairly traditional, with mixed planting of shrubs, herbaceous, bulbs, and so on, using soft colours
- include a range of evergreen shrubs to screen out panel fences and to provide foliage for cutting
- small-flowered clematis, for example viticella cvs, to grow through some of the shrubs
- create planting for winter interest in bed nearest the back door
- all planting to be relatively low maintenance; no staking of herbaceous plants
- must include some plants for year-round interest and colour
- wants at least two shrub roses, preferred colours deep/pale pink, and they must have perfume
- lavender to be planted around seating area
- incorporate some grasses and easy to maintain herbaceous plants for summer colour
- avoid orange flowers
- use a range of spring-flowering bulbs
- make suggestions for spring and summer colour schemes and plant lists for existing containers

gardens and the law

Whether you are working in your own or a client's garden it is important to know something about garden law in their area. Such laws can be very complicated, and will vary from country to country and in federal countries such as the United States from one state to another. It is not only site boundaries that are likely to be controlled by the law but also some of the plants growing within them.

Site boundaries

Unfortunately boundaries, especially hedges and fences, can quite often be the cause of disputes between neighbours. You therefore need to know who owns which boundary of a property, because owners are responsible for the upkeep of their boundaries. If you or your client is not sure, then ask the neighbours; it may also be worth checking the property deeds because ownership may be marked on these. If in doubt you sould seek local advice before undertaking any work that could result in a court case.

Another reason to understand garden law is that a dispute could arise if one neighbour fails to maintain their fence and as a result of this their dog or other pet gets through into the next door neighbour's garden and does a considerable amount of damage. This could result in considerable unpleasantness or even a court case.

Plants growing alongside boundaries, or when they are used to create the boundary itself, can create maintenance for the neighbours and so become a source of disputes. A hedge growing along the boundary between two properties, for example, is normally the responsibility of both neighbours, but a problem may arise when one neighbour does not keep their side of the hedge trimmed and this affects the amount of sunlight that can reach the neighbour's garden.

If a hedge belonging to one neighbour grows into the adjacent garden, the neighbour is entitled to invite the hedge owner to come round and cut it, or they can prune it themselves. As trees mature they too may encroach onto another's property with their branches or roots. The law usually allows the adjoining landowner to cut off any branch that crosses his or her boundary without notice to the owner of the tree. However, branches must never be cut back farther than the boundary line – regardless of what may be the best arboricultural practice. Take professional advice before cutting any cross-boundary tree roots causing damage to property, because the law may not take the same view as you as to the source of the damage to your property. The owner of a tree may in fact be liable for any damage by the encroaching tree roots caused to a neighbouring property. Permission must always be sought before entering your neighbour's land in order to prune your (not their tree) tree or collect fruit from it.

There is no obligation under law for an owner to cut a hedge or prune a tree growing near but not overhanging the boundary of their property, however much the neighbouring landowner may object to it.

Plants adjacent to a road

Where a tree, hedge, or shrub overhanging a road or pavement causes danger by obstructing vehicles or pedestrians or interfering with the view of drivers, then the local authority may give notice to the owner to cut the plant to remove the danger. If the owner fails to comply, the authority may do the work and charge the owner. The owner of a tree may also be responsible to a third party if branches, roots, or timber rot cause an accident and the owner can be proved negligent in any way.

The status of trees

Before you begin work on any site take time to find out about the status of any trees on that site. It may be that some of the mature trees are legally protected because they are of value in the immediate area. They may be

especially beautiful, particularly rare or old, provide an excellent wildlife habitat, or grow in a conservation area. They may also be legally protected if they screen out an eyesore or future development. Such a tree should normally be visible from a public place, although in a private garden it may be seen only from the surrounding houses.

Any legally protected trees cannot be felled, and you will have to get permission to do any work on them. You should be able to get information and a list of protected trees from your local planning office. If the owner of a protected tree fails to get permission for any work to be done, then he or she is likely to incur a large fine.

If you are ever in doubt about the health or safety of any tree on site, you should contact a qualified tree surgeon (arborist). This is also important if any work, such as hard landscaping, is to be carried out that could affect changes in soil level near an existing tree. A good starting point would be a phone call to the local tree officer or a surveyor.

It is always worth trying to keep any suitable mature trees and incorporate them into your design. Trees take a considerable amount of time to grow and frequently some careful pruning by a qualified tree surgeon as well as some regular maintenance can restore a tree to its former glory and set it up for a healthy future.

Boundary plants

ABOVE LEFT Trees and hedges growing on or alongside boundaries may easily become the cause of disputes between neighbours if they are not adequately maintained by both parties.

Structural damage

ABOVE RIGHT The roots of large trees may be the cause of structural damage to walls and buildings. Seek professional advice from an arborist and structural engineer before removing a tree, especially when it is growing in clay soil.

where to get your plants

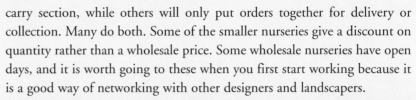

Most gardeners enjoy buying plants for their own gardens, and in the process visit a variety of garden centres and nurseries. When you start working professionally, you will not be able to do this for every client so it is essential that you build up a list of reliable wholesale and retail nurseries that are able to supply you with a good range of quality plants. Many nurseries have websites and online catalogues so it is easy to view the range of plants they can supply. Before ordering any plants for the first time, try to visit their nursery so that you can see for yourself the quality and range of plants.

There are many different types of nurseries, and it is normally fairly easy to source trees and shrubs from a local wholesale one. It can be more difficult to find a good range of roses, herbaceous plants, grasses, and ferns, and you will often need to go directly to a specialist nursery for these. Once you have located these specialists, and are happy with the quality of plants they supply, try to work from their plant lists or catalogue when doing planting plans then you know you can source the plants.

Wholesale nurseries do not usually sell to the general public, and you will probably need to show a business card on your first visit. Some of them operate a cash-and-

carry section, while others will only put orders together for delivery or collection. Many do both. Some of the smaller nurseries give a discount on quantity rather than a wholesale price. Some wholesale nurseries have open days, and it is worth going to these when you first start working because it is a good way of networking with other designers and landscapers.

Trees and shrubs may be bought container grown, bare-root, or rootballed. Container grown are the most popular, because these can in theory be planted at any time of the year. Bare-root plants are the cheapest way of buying deciduous trees and shrubs, particularly hedging, or when large quantities are required. They are grown in open ground and lifted and planted during the dormant season. Evergreens such as conifers and rhododendrons that have shallow fibrous roots are sold rootballed, as are large specimen trees. These are lifted from open ground by machines and the roots and soil are wrapped in netting. Once lifted, they need to be plunged into beds of organic matter to stop the roots and soil from drying out until they can be planted.

Smaller plants should grow away quickly and can be a good choice when maintenance is limited. However, larger specimens create more immediate impact. These days there is a vast range of trees and shrubs that can be supplied as mature specimens. They tend to be expensive, and very often the nursery will offer a planting service for large trees together with the assurance that they will be replaced in event of failure to thrive in their new surroundings.

It is always best to be on site when an order is delivered so that you can check it and send any inferior plants back to the nursery with a request for replacements (see p.179).

Nursery stock

LEFT Only buy plants that have been well maintained.
1   A range of sun-loving plants laid out in alphabetical order
2   A shade house for plants that cannot take full sun
3   Examples of clipped box and topiary
4   Shrubs used for propagation set out in stock beds

Bedding plants

RIGHT Plants used for seasonal bedding can either be bought in small individual pots or more economically in trays (as shown here).

plant and pot sizes

It takes a little while to become familiar with plant and pot sizes, and it is worth taking time to visit wholesale and retail nurseries so that you are aware of the range of plants that each supplies.

Tree sizes

When ordering a tree you need to specify the size, that is its stem size and height. In Europe trees are measured by girth size in centimetres. This measurement is taken 1m (3ft) from ground level and is the circumference of the trunk at this point. The girth measurement will normally also equate to an approximate height, so if a tree has a girth of 10–12cm (4–5in) it would probably have a clear stem of 2.1–2.7m (7–9ft) before the head branches out. The container size may also be quoted in litres.

In the USA tree sizes are measured by caliper in inches. This measurement is the diameter of the trunk 15cm (6in) above ground level up to 10cm (4in) caliper size; for anything over 10cm (4in) it is measured 30cm (12in) above ground level. The height of the clear stem (in feet) from ground level will also be stated.

Before ordering a large tree do check whether it is actually possible to get the tree on site, because the only access to the garden could be through the house or a narrow side passage. Large trees also require secure anchorage and very regular watering once they have been planted. A piece of plastic pipe alongside a mature tree will direct any water down to the roots.

Buying shrubs and herbaceous plants

Shrubs and herbaceous plants are normally sold by container size, and this is stated as a volume. In Europe the containers for shrubs are always in litres, while in the USA they are according to container class: for example, # 1 or #14, which equates to volume in cubic inches. Some of the smaller shrubs such as lavenders and hebes are only available in small containers –

1–2 litres (#SP4– #SP5). Meanwhile herbaceous plants are also sold in these smaller container sizes because they are generally planted in drifts or groups and small plants establish and grow away quicker than larger ones, soon creating an effective planting.

When ordering plants it is usual to choose smaller-sized pots – 2, 3, and 5 litres (#SP4, #SP5, and #2) – and then select a few larger plants to create some instant impact. Bare-rooted plants must be heeled in if they are not going to be planted immediately otherwise the root hairs will dry out.

Buying trees
LEFT AND BELOW Trees are sold by stem height and girth (or caliper in the US).

deep pot

rootballed plant

Deep pot
LEFT Climbers are sold in extra-long pots, which give the supporting cane some stability.

Buying plants
ABOVE European container sizes roughly equate to US container-class ones.

1 1 litre/#SP4
2 2 litres/#SP5
3 3 litres/#1
4 5 litres/#2
5 7.5 litres/#2
5 10 litres/#3
7 15 litres/#5
8 20 litres/#5

Rootball plant
ABOVE RIGHT Such trees or shrubs can be very heavy for one person to handle, and they need an extra large planting hole.

plant schedules

If you are designing more than one garden then plant schedules soon become an important part of your business documentation. Writing a plant schedule can seem an onerous task at first, but once you become more familiar with nurseries and plant supply it quickly becomes just another part of the job. It needs to be professionally presented, so do check all plant nomenclature carefully against the relevant nursery catalogue before sending lists off to the nursery or the client.

A plant schedule is prepared in conjunction with the planting plan, and it lists all the plants that you have included in your scheme. The easiest way to prepare a plant schedule is to compile the list at the same time as you ink up your planting plan otherwise it is easy to miss a group of plants. The schedule is then used to order and cost the plants. Many people enjoy ordering the plants, while others prefer to leave it to a contractor.

The plant schedule needs to have a front cover. This states who the schedule is for (that is, the client's name) and that it should be read in conjunction with planting plan number 5532 (or however you have numbered the job). Like the report front cover (see p.171), it also needs to include your name, address, contact details, and a date.

If the schedule is for only a small garden or area of planting, all the plants can simply be listed alphabetically under the headings of trees, shrubs, climbing plants, herbaceous perennials, bulbs, and so on. You must state the number of each plant that you require and its size, using girth for trees and pot size in litres for the other plants. In a large garden it is easier to identify the beds or areas of planting by letters or numbers and then prepare lists for each of these in turn under the same headings of trees, shrubs, and so on. This makes it considerably easier to sort the plants out into the appropriate bed or area of the garden once you are ready to start planting up.

Before sending a plant list off to the nursery for a quotation, it is a good idea to check that there is a clause in your plant schedule stating that no substitutes are to be supplied unless agreed with the designer. Also allow space on the right-hand side of the schedule for the nursery to add their price. If you are sourcing your plants from more than one supplier, you need to prepare a separate plant schedule for each nursery.

Nurseries will usually give the net price so you have to add any national or local sales tax to this as well as a mark-up of whatever percentage you deem appropriate. You then give this final price to the client as the quotation for the plants.

Coordinating planting times

Some plants such as bulbs or bare-root plants will be delivered only at very particular times of year, and it is difficult to plant trees once all the other planting has gone in. You should therefore aim to delay all the planting until the dormant season or else buy trees container grown rather than bare-root and make sure they are well watered throughout the first year.

PLANT SCHEDULE (for planting plan 5532)

NAME	QUANTITY	SIZE	NURSERY QUOTE	
Trees			Unit price	Total
		Girth/caliper and height		
Amelanchier lamarckii	1	Container grown 8–10cm girth		
Prunus avium	1	Bare-root 10–12cm girth		
Shrubs		Container size/ class		
Abelia × *grandiflora*	1	3 litres		
Buxus sempervirens	6	3 litres		
Choisya ternata	2	5 litres		
Lavandula pedunculata				

CHECKS TO BE MADE ON PLANTS

When your plant order is delivered it is worth taking time to check over the plants very carefully before accepting delivery. Carry out the following quality checks:

- that you are the addressee of the order.
- all the plants are clearly labelled.
- you have received the correct number and specified size of each plant.
- any substitutes have been cleared with you well before delivery takes place.
- the compost is clean and free of weeds and liverworts.
- the plants look healthy and free of pests and diseases.
- plants are not damaged.
- pots are not broken.
- the condition of the compost; if dry, water immediately.
- if there are any bare-root plants; if so, they should be heeled in until you are ready to plant.

Checking the plants

FAR RIGHT Make sure you are on hand when the plants are delivered so that you can tick them off against the original order. You will probably require help if any large container plants (right) are to be moved once they are on site.

schedule of work

A schedule of work is really like an action plan for carrying out any project, and it will help you to see clearly how much work is involved and also the costs. Such a schedule for your own garden might be a loosely drawn-up series of worksheets which you can add to, and make notes on, as you go along.

This detailed programme describes how to do the work for each design job, and the materials to be used. It does not really matter how you write it initially, but if you are going to get someone else to do the work for you then the final document needs to be easy to use with a logical structure, and should be in clear, concise language.

Writing a schedule of work

The best approach is to think yourself through the project and list all the stages of work involved. You can then put these into a logical sequence and include details on materials and exactly how the job should be carried out. At the same time you can create a separate list of all the materials and tools that will be required, and this will help you to estimate the cost of the project. If you have a large garden then you may need to break the schedule of work down into individual areas.

You should always start the schedule with some general preambles about the site, working hours, health and safety issues while on site, and anything else that you feel is relevant for the overall successful implementation of the scheme. It should then cover in detail everything from the start to the finish of the job and include topics such as start and end dates, preparing the ground, planting, clearing away rubbish, and leaving the site clean and tidy. If you set your notes up as separate points on your computer and number them in a logical manner, then you can use them for more than one job. The points should be written as instructions, as though you are telling someone else how to do the work.

The first main heading in the schedule of work should be site clearance. Under this you note details about how you intend to get rid of any perennial weeds such as ground elder or bindweed and in what way you intend to dispose of large woody plants being removed from the site.

You can then create a schedule for the preparation of the beds. List the materials you need to buy, such as well-rotted farmyard manure and fertilizer, and work out the quantities and cost. You should describe how the soil is to be dug, weeds to be removed, and soil improved by the addition of organic matter (which you have already noted to buy). You also need to include ordering of the plants so that they are delivered only once the beds have been prepared.

The remaining headings in the schedule of work should include:

- delivery of plants – check all plants correspond to those on the plant schedule, are in good condition, true to name, free of pests and diseases, and that they are watered on arrival, if appropriate.
- setting out – the way in which plants are to be arranged (as noted in the planting plan).
- planting – detailed instructions on how to plant and stake trees, shrubs, herbaceous plants, and bulbs. Include a reminder that plants should be placed with their best side towards the front, and that they require watering and mulching. Also describe how to plant climbers or wall shrubs (if appropriate) and what type of support such as trellis they need (check support and wire are on the items-to-buy list).
- aftercare of all plants – watering, pruning, feeding.
- notes on how the site should be left – all rubbish disposed of, pots cleared away, lawn area made good; area left clean and tidy.

If you then receive more design commisions, you will find these notes invaluable, and they can be worked up into a more professional document.

SITE CLEARANCE

Items to buy
- wheelbarrow
- plastic sheeting to protect lawn and paved areas
- sheet of ply in case ground is wet or maybe some boards (find out cost of these)
- spade and fork (already have one of each)
- garden rake
- plant pots (already have sufficient for this job)
- hose 30m (100ft) and reel, plus adaptor for outside tap and spray attachment

Site preparation
- order skip for [insert proposed start date]
- list any trees or shrubs that are to remain in situ and label them clearly
- list and label herbaceous plants that are to be kept
- clear garage to give easy access to front garden
- clear area at bottom of garden as plant-holding area. Make sure hose will reach this area
- protect lawn and paved areas with plastic sheeting or boards
- if ground is wet do not wheel the barrow across the lawn without putting boards down
- ensure all spades and forks are pushed into ground when not in use and that the rake is laid with prongs in the ground or stood upright against a fence

Bed clearance
- make a potting compost mix with peat-based compost and John Innes No 2.
- lift any herbaceous plants that are labelled, and pot up using prepared potting compost
- water plants and move to prepared area at end of garden; keep well watered
- clear all remaining unwanted plants ensuring complete removal of all roots
- place all roots and large woody branches in the skip
- put small woody and green material on the compost heap
- double-check that all remaining shrubs are labelled "to be kept". Review their shape and consider whether they are still wanted and if so whether they need pruning. Do this before starting the bed preparation
- clear away debris, sweep up, and leave site clean and tidy at end of each day
- clean tools and put them away in shed

Basic preparation
ABOVE Before starting to lift the plants and clear the bed put a plastic sheet down to protect the grass. Also ensure that you have all the tools and other items that you will need. Take care to push spades and forks into the ground when not in use to prevent accidents.

Coping with drought
LEFT In very dry weather you may need to soak the ground well before trying to lift plants that you want to keep. It may also be necessary to irrigate new planting regularly to aid its survival.

maintenance schedule

Gardens are generally very contrived environments that need regular maintenance if they are going to flourish. And to anyone who has little or no gardening experience it can seem quite daunting to look after a newly planted garden filled with plants bearing complicated Latin names. Starting with your own garden, it can therefore be a very useful exercise to draw up a maintenance schedule listing all the tasks that need to be carried out during the year. There are various way of producing such an annual maintenance schedule, but the simplest is probably to create a table that shows tasks to be done in each season (or by month of the year).

Maintenance factsheets

It is also helpful to write some factsheets on specific topics such as shrub pruning, annual lawn maintenance, border maintenance, tree care, and planting up containers. You can then use these detailed sheets alongside the annual maintenance schedule. The tasks in a factsheet will vary slightly from project to project, but for example one on shrub pruning will most likely include the following information.

Shrub pruning is fairly complex, so its factsheet is best done by creating groups and then explaining how to prune plants in each group. These might comprise:

Group 1 – evergreen shrubs that require little regular pruning
Group 2 – deciduous shrubs pruned in late winter/early spring
Group 3 – deciduous shrubs pruned in early summer after flowering
Group 4 – shrubs that are pollarded or coppiced in early spring

The factsheet also needs to include some clear diagrams of before and after pruning a shrub within each group. Within the annual maintenance schedule you can then list the shrubs in the garden and refer back to the pruning factsheet for appropriate details: for example, *Abelia* x *grandiflora* Group 2; *Buddleja davidii* Group 2; *Cornus alba* 'Sibirica' Group 4; *Weigela* 'Florida Variegata' Group 3; *Viburnum tinus* Group 1.

A factsheet for border maintenance would give details on application rates for each type of fertilizer, how and when to mulch, and how to look after herbaceous plants and grasses in the garden.

Producing an annual maintenance schedule is very time-consuming, but like other business documentation the schedule can be adapted to any number of projects or clients. If you are preparing a maintenance schedule or giving factsheets to a client then you should charge for this service.

Necessary care
LEFT Beds and borders need to be regularly maintained. Weeds compete with plants for moisture, nutrients, and light, and the more vigorous plants will eventually smother other plants if not kept in check by regular pruning.

TASKS FOR INCLUSION IN A MAINTENANCE SCHEDULE

Border maintenance
Weeding
Feeding
Mulching
Staking herbaceous plants
Shrub pruning – prepare separate
factsheet on pruning
Protection from pests and diseases
Lifting and dividing of herbaceous
plants
Cutting down to ground level

Lawn maintenance
Scarification
Aeration
Topdressing
Weeding
Feeding
Mowing
Edging
Repair

**Maintenance for wall shrubs
and climbers**
Training and tying in
Mulching
Pruning

Tree maintenance
Formative pruning
Watering
Weeding
Mulching
Checking ties and stakes

EXAMPLE OF ANNUAL MAINTENANCE SCHEDULE

TASK	Lawn maintenance Refer to factsheet for details	Shrub pruning Refer to factsheet and list of shrubs for details	Border maintenance Refer to relevant factsheets and plant lists for details
midwinter			Clear leaves and debris. Tidy evergreen leaves
late winter	Rake lawn	Prune shrubs in Group 2	Clear leaves. Cut back remaining herbaceous plants/grasses
early spring	Rake lawn. First cut slightly higher than normal. Repair edges	Prune shrubs in Group 4	Fork over border. Weed, feed, and mulch
midspring	Feed and weed. Mow	Prune shrubs in Group 1 as necessary	Weed and tidy. Remove faded evergreen leaves
late spring	Mow		Weed. Stake herbaceous plants. Watch for pests and diseases
early summer	Mow and neaten lawn edges as required throughout summer	Prune shrubs in Group 3	Weed. Deadhead. Cut back plants that have finished flowering
midsummer			Weed. Deadhead. Cut back as appropriate. Tie in tall plants
late summer		Prune grey-leaved shrubs in Group 1 as necessary	Continue to weed. Deadhead, cut back, tidy
early autumn			
midautumn	Scarify. Aerate. Feed. Topdress		
late autumn	Rake leaves		Clear leaves. Cut some herbaceous plants down to ground level
early winter	Rake leaves		Clear leaves. Lift and divide herbaceous plants

costings

When you first start to work for clients you will find it very difficult to know how much to charge, because your own labour costs are particularly difficult to judge. If you have recently planted up your own garden, you may have some record of the cost of plants and materials and if you employed someone to help then you will be aware, too, of how much they charged. You also need to include in your charges all the hidden costs in running a business such as heating your office, running your car, telephone and broadband charges, computer paper, and ink cartridges.

Generally you can consider costs under these headings: Initial client visit; Planting plan; Plants; Materials; and Labour. It is usual to charge an hourly rate for the initial visit, and a fixed price for the planting plan based on how long you think it will take. Work out a daily rate for yourself, and if you keep a record of the time you spend at the drawing board, then you will soon see how your time is taken up.

Plants

Fortunately, it is relatively easy to arrive at a cost for the plants (see p.178). If the nursery has labelled the plants with the wholesale price, you should remove these before the plants arrive on site. It is good practice to replace plants if they fail within a specified time, but this must be on the understanding that clients have followed your aftercare instructions, especially on watering.

Materials

There will always be a range of other materials needed when implementing a planting scheme, and it is usual to mark up the price of these by 30–40 percent if you are buying them at trade price.

Organic matter such as well-rotted farmyard manure or spent mushroom compost is usually applied at a depth of about 10cm (4in) throughout the border, so 1 cu m will cover 10 sq m (1 cu yd for 9.2 sq yd). Calculate how many square metres (square yards) the planting area covers, so you can work out the cost to the client. The application rate and depth of organic mulches such as shredded bark are similar to farmyard manure. There is no standard depth for an inorganic mulch such as gravel, so these costs must be researched with care.

If you offer garden maintenance services as well as planting ones, you probably need a range of different fertilizers for base and top dressings and also spring and autumn lawn feeds. These are expensive when bought at garden centres so try to find an alternate source offering wholesale prices.

Other items could include tree stakes and ties, wire, vine eyes, twine, staples, and trellis panels. If a skip is being ordered then this must be included in the cost together with a permit if it has to be left on the road. Sometimes you also have to pay to park your vehicles near the site.

Labour

Probably the most difficult cost to work out is labour, because in order to charge the right amount you need to gauge fairly accurately how long a job is going to take. Always build some flexibility into your time schedule because setting out and planting generally take longer then expected. Remember to allow time for clearing up and watering at the end of each day and when you have finished the whole job. You may also want to employ someone to help with the heavy digging and preparation work.

Try to quote a daily rate rather than an hourly rate for labour, and as you should be on site to set the plants out and help with the planting you need to decide on a daily rate for yourself as well. This will be less than the rate you charge when you are working as a designer. If you intend to make a follow-up visit to see how the plants are doing, then that also needs to be included in the final client costings.

Price and size

RIGHT The client's budget will affect the size of the plants that can be bought. Large palms such as those illustrated here are very expensive, so it may be cost-effective to buy only one or two large plants for creating real immediate impact.

glossary

Aspect – the orientation of the garden: north, south, east, or west.

Asymmetrical design – when each side of the garden or planting is different.

Bulb – a modified stem acting as a storage organ, consisting of fleshy, tightly packed leaves on a much reduced stem.

Calcicole – a plant that thrives in alkaline soil (above pH 7).

Calcifuge – a plant that requires acid soil of pH 4.0–5.5; it will not grow in alkaline soil.

Chlorosis – the yellowing of leaves caused by an iron or magnesium deficiency.

Corm – an underground storage organ comprising a swollen stem, which is renewed annually.

Cultivar – a contraction of "cultivated variety" – a plant that has been produced by plant breeders and will not reproduce itself exactly from seed.

Deciduous – a tree or shrub that loses its leaves at the end of the growing season and renews them at the beginning of the next.

Ecological planting – the use of only those plants that will thrive in particular growing conditions; often referred to as "right plant, right place".

Ericaceous – plants in family Ericaceae; they are usually lime-hating and require acid soil below pH 6.5.

Evergreen – plants that retain their foliage for more than one growing season.

Form – the three-dimensional (3D) shape of a plant when clad in foliage.

Formative pruning – a method of pruning that is carried out on young trees and shrubs so they possess a good shape when mature.

Frost pocket – a site, often a hollow where cold air gathers, that is subject to severe and often prolonged bouts of frost.

Genus – a category in plant classification ranked between family and species; a group of related species linked by a range of common characteristics.

Glaucous foliage – blue-green or blue-grey leaves.

Half-hardy – able to withstand temperatures down to freezing point (0°C/32°F).

Hardy – able to withstand year-round growing conditions including frost.

Heeling in – planting temporarily until a plant can be placed in its permanent site.

Herbaceous plant – a non-woody plant in which the upper parts die down to a rootstock at the end of the growing season; chiefly applied to perennials.

Hybrid – the offspring of genetically different parents. Hybrids between species are known as inter-specific hybrids. Those between different genera are inter-generic hybrids.

Iron sequestrene – an available form of iron that can be added to alkaline soil to prevent chlorosis in ericaceous (acid-loving) plants.

John Innes compost – loam-based potting compost devised by the John Innes Horticultural Institute (UK) and made to a standard formula.

Knot garden – beds laid out in a formal often complex pattern formed from dwarf hedges or clipped herbs.

Mulch – a material applied in a thick layer to the soil surface to suppress weeds and conserve moisture.

Naturalize – establish and grow a plant as if in the wild.

Nutrients – minerals used to produce compounds required for plant growth.

Perennial – any plant living for more than three years; commonly applied to herbaceous plants and woody perennials, that is, trees and shrubs.

pH – a measure of alkalinity or acidity used horticulturally to refer to soils; the scale measures from 1 (acid) to 14 (alkaline) with 7 as neutral.

Pleaching – a technique whereby branches from a row of trees are woven together and trained to form a wall or canopy of foliage.